Loving
at a Distance

THE GERMAN LIST

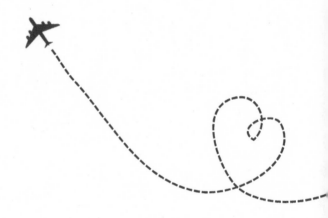

Petra Hardt

Rights

Buying, Protecting, Selling

Translated by Jeremy Gaines

PETRA HARDT

Loving
at a Distance

TRANSLATED BY
LAURA WAGNER

LONDON NEW YORK CALCUTTA

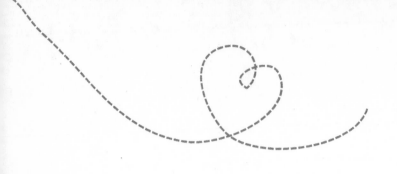

GOETHE
INSTITUT

This publication has been supported by a
grant from the Goethe-Institut India

Seagull Books, 2022

First published in German as *Fernlieben* by Petra Hardt
© Insel Verlag, Berlin, 2021

First published in English translation by Seagull Books, 2022
English translation © Laura Wagner, 2022

ISBN   978 1 8030 9 028 3

British Library Cataloguing-in-Publication Data
A catalogue record for this book is available from the British Library.

Typeset by Seagull Books, Calcutta, India
Printed and bound in the USA by Integrated Books International

For
Annaliese, Klaus, Gesa,
Ruth, Barry, Linda, Alicia, Geeta,
Ellen, Christine, Bine, Charly

&

my grandchildren
Leonora, Quentin, Emilia, Nora

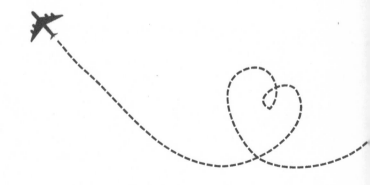

CONTENTS

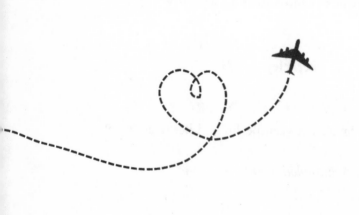

Preface to the English Edition

In this book I talk about distance—physical distance, in particular. Sociologists Eva Illouz, Ulrich Beck, and Elisabeth Beck-Gernsheim have studied the idea of distance and how global living and working conditions affect small and large social units.

This is not a new aspect of communal existence. For centuries people have migrated between continents—in ideal circumstances, their movement was voluntarily—to find a way of life that would guarantee freedom and prosperity.

After the personal experience of a close family member leaving Europe to study, work, and live in the United States of America, I gained a clearer view of migration and the consequences it entails. My visits to the United States revealed my linguistic and cognitive deficiencies. My understanding of the very diverse American society evolved over the years with each stay, but so did the realization that migration processes take decades.

I first became interested in exploring the notion of distance because of migration within my family. But then my observations shifted from private transatlantic travel between Germany and the United States to the countries I visited in a professional capacity. I realized that I carried a magnifying glass through which I observed social processes around me at all times. And that it influenced the way I worked with texts. Through personal experience, I gained a greater sensitivity for the book trade with other countries—illustrated by four examples discussed in this volume.

Loving at a Distance was written between March and July 2020. Since then, the SARS-CoV-2 virus has gripped the global population. Iconic images of people holding, embracing one another after eighteen months of separation have traveled around the world. The culture and media sector, which includes the book trade and the dissemination of literature and science, were forced into a standstill for long stretches of time. Some of the major international book fairs took place online and showed that both love and the conversation about literature require nearness. *Loving at a Distance* describes how global lifestyles created by climatic and political changes influence our coexistence. The balance of nearness and distance will have to be newly defined for the humankind.

January 2022

Loving
at a Distance

I

Berkeley

Playing with my grandchildren is my favorite thing to do. They live in Berkeley, California, and I live in Berlin. Twice a year I fly across Iceland, Greenland, and Canada to see my family in the US. My friends say: *You're such a great fit for Berkeley.* I disagree: I'm neither an aging hippie nor a member of the Jewish or Hispanic community or associated with the university. Apart from the time I spend with my grandchildren, I feel alone. Before they moved to Berkeley, the children lived in Menlo Park, south of San Francisco, for five years. My friends said: *You're such a great fit for Menlo Park.* I disagree: I'm over forty, I don't work for Google/Alphabet, Amazon, Apple, or Facebook/Meta, I don't drive a Tesla or a coupe and only occasionally eat vegan. Clichés all around. Structures that are foreign and remain foreign to me. That work equally perfectly in Berkeley and in Menlo Park. Anyone who describes a unified global culture of the digital age probably never stayed in one place for very long. You need at least a decade to really arrive in a foreign city.

I miss Ulrich Beck. "Love at a Distance: The Chaos of Global Relationships" was one of his areas of research. In 2011, he and his wife Elisabeth Beck-Gernsheim wrote a book by the same name. He died much too young. I would ask him to add to his book. "Loving at a distance" begins with Skype and continues at airports. The destination airport becomes a Mecca. In both directions. For the emigrants and the family that stays back in the home country.

Rarely have I experienced foreignness as strongly as in Stavanger, Norway. In the evenings, the natives retreat to their homes, having long since been forced to give up their hospitality in the face of countless Asian and African oil-rig workers along with the daily onslaught of around two thousand cruise-ship passengers. The beautiful city, with Europe's largest and oldest settlement of wooden houses, is being overwhelmed by two-hour tourism and the global oil industry. The African and Asian oil workers at the harbor look inward. Tragic scenes play out at Stavanger Airport as parents say goodbye to their children who are returning home with their grandparents while the breadwinners stay in Norway. How can you bear it? I wonder. All it takes for me to get stressed is an interruption in the digital communication with my grandchildren in California. Waiting for the next conversation on Skype or FaceTime, the expected parcel containing the grandchildren's drawings, the next WhatsApp message, the pictures uploaded to the private family Twitter account, the video on Marco Polo—these are all parts of my daily routine. The different time zones have long since become firmly anchored within the soul. Friends say: *You're going to settle in California easily.* For a person of my generation that grew up in West Germany, I was late in reaching the West Coast of the United States. I was already fifty-six when I came to San Francisco for the first time. My friends traveled to California in the 1970s, hung out in San Francisco or Monterey and drove along Route 66. After graduating high school, I visited Italy and France. Is there a connection between the personal sentiment of feeling foreign in California and my age? Or do the students at the University of California, Berkeley, feel the same?

On the morning of my arrival in Berkeley in February 2018, I walk across the campus to the Charles Franklin Doe Library. An exhibition is advertised in the entrance hall: "Reframing Aging"—photographs and stories of people between the ages of seventy and ninety-six. The exhibition is being sponsored by Ashby Village, a non-profit that brings together elderly people with shared interests from Monday to Friday every week. I register my new interest in the elderly with some skepticism. I suspect that it is related to my impending retirement. Only five years earlier I had made fun of anti-aging products in a questionnaire for *Börsenblatt*, the trade journal of the German book-publishing industry. Since then, I have watched all seven seasons of *Grace and Frankie* as well as all three seasons of *The Kominsky Method* on Netflix.

Looking at the exhibition, I remember my first visit to the campus of the world-famous UC Berkeley a few years ago. I had scheduled a three-hour window to visit the campus and the campanile. I went to the Visitor Center, got the necessary maps, and inquired where I could find the philosophy department. I asked for traces of Adorno. Theodor W. Adorno had established a cooperation with the Berkeley Public Opinion Study Group when he lived in his Santa Monica exile in the 1940s and occasionally traveled from Los Angeles to UC Berkeley. I admit, my wish to see plaques commemorating the Frankfurt School in the philosophy department was a little presumptuous. The friendly student working at the reception desk was unfamiliar with the name Theodor W. Adorno, and asked tersely, "You are interested in philosophy?"

Silicon Valley

In 1998, when Steve Jobs became a global player with Apple twenty-two years after founding the company, and Larry Page and Sergey Brin set up Google in Menlo Park, I was living in the hills of Taunus with my family and drove along the A66 every morning to my office at Suhrkamp Publishing House in Frankfurt and back home in the afternoons. What was happening in Silicon Valley wasn't relevant to us at the time. We were just getting used to working with computers, data storage and processing capacities, and the internet at our workplaces. We were stragglers. We suspected that the products from Silicon Valley were going to completely recalibrate our lives, but we didn't know for sure. When I traveled to the Bay Area, south of San Francisco, to the so-called Silicon Valley for the first time in 2010, Google had moved from Menlo Park to Mountain View, and the Valley had become the most important producer of digital technologies in the world.

The headquarters of the IT giants have formed their own cities in the rather small towns of the Bay Area. The most spectacular, and most secluded, is Norman Foster's Apple Park in Cupertino. Facebook/Meta headquarters are between the Bayshore Freeway and the Bayfront Expressway in Menlo Park. I drove past them twice a day to bring my granddaughter to day-care and to pick her up again. The colorful townhouses and buildings in the company premises between the two freeways are meant to convey comfort. But they don't. There are better things. Like the grand country house with its own park at the corner of Glenwood Avenue and Middlefield Road in Menlo Park. It was sold through Sotheby's in September 2016. Just the year before, it had been lavishly lit and decorated for Christmas. I was certain: a happy family lives there. The children in blue blazers, a Cabernet Sauvignon from the Napa Valley, and the Dow Jones favorable. The new McEwan from Kepler's bookstore on the table with the presents. Maybe the happy family found a bigger house among the hills between San Francisco and the Pacific. But maybe the family wasn't all that happy after all. Just like the family of acquaintances in Königstein im Taunus with children in blue blazers. In their case, the family court decided that the parents could only see each other from hundred metres apart. In that house they could have managed to do so even without a judge's orders.

I am waiting in a long queue with my granddaughter in front of Sushirrito, a restaurant on University Avenue in Palo Alto, at lunchtime: Mega Sushi, XXL Sushi; Ten Types of Sushi as Big as a Burrito—Geisha's Kiss with Tuna; Sumo

Crunch with Crabmeat. The options also include Mayan Dragon, Buddha Belly, and Salmon Samba. We share a Sumo Crunch with Crabmeat. After lunch we go to the playground in Burgess Park, which borders the stunning creek that runs through Palo Alto. The park offers large lawns, an outdoor swimming pool, training grounds for baseball, basketball, and skateboarding. On the weekends, many families come here to have barbeques or to celebrate children's birthday parties. My granddaughter is on the swings. Next to her is a child whose Asian grandmother sings American children's songs tunefully. So far, my granddaughter only knows German children's songs. But we're not going to sing those aloud in Burgess Park. On the way home I stop at Kepler's and buy three songbooks with the most famous American children's songs, including a CD. One would have been enough, my son says. The international community that has settled here plays in the Silicon Valley parks. The children in the Bay Area grow up with at least two languages. English and the respective native language. I only ever speak German with my grandchildren, while the children switch between English and German effortlessly, depending on what the situation requires. The two languages with which we move through the Bay Area create two realities. My grandchildren's generation is growing up in a world that I will only experience partly. It is the finitude that makes bearable this Valley of endless opportunities.

In the evenings I sometimes go to the restaurant Bird Dog in Palo Alto with friends—a couple—who teach at Stanford. Born in Germany between 1948 and 1960, gathered here in the Valley: the emigrants who have become American citizens, and the visitor. The couple has long left behind the foreignness that I feel in the Valley. The anxiety about what is to come is bigger than our equanimity. I think about Elizabeth Strout who writes in her novel *Olive, Again*: "To bear the burden of the mystery with as much grace as we can." Such sentences encourage an attitude, and I feel I'm particularly receptive to them.

The next day my granddaughter and I drive to have lunch with her parents at the Google/Alphabet headquarters on Amphitheater Parkway in Mountain View. At the entrance a sign reads: *Please be Google. All guests must be registered and wearing a visitor's badge prior to entering a Google facility. Even grandmas and the kids.*

I say to my grandchild: "They put up that sign because of us." I take note of the fact that corporate management puts grandmothers and children in the same risk category. Forty thousand employees work on the premises. A city with large buildings, most of them four stories tall because of regulations. A huge campus with parks, palm trees, canteens, cafes, pools, sports facilities, everything in Google's colors. Many Indian and Asian families are visiting the company but none of them are grandmothers. I assert my dominant position, but no one takes any notice. The food at Google is good, generous, and rich in variety. All requirements—vegan, vegetarian, Asian, American—are catered for. But it's not as good as the food at Twitter in San Francisco. Rarely have I eaten as well as I did at Twitter. But they only have four thousand employees to cook for. I haven't eaten at Facebook yet—don't have any friends there.

Creaking grey trains called Caltrains operated by Transit-America Services run through the Valley and transport hundreds of thousands of commuters from San Francisco, Albany, Richmond, Berkeley, Oakland to Palo Alto, Mountain View, Cupertino; to Apple, Hewlett-Packard, Google, eBay, Twitter, Facebook, Yahoo, Adobe; to the stores of SAP, Microsoft, Nokia, Amazon and a hundred more world-famous tech companies and five hundred lesser-known internet companies and start-ups; and to the research institutions in Stanford and Berkeley. Depending on their size, the trains reserve three or four carriages exclusively for bicycles. The screeching brakes at the twenty-three stops, the bell-like announcement of the trains: an anachronism in the valley of digital top speed.

On our way to Menlo Park my granddaughter falls asleep. I keep on driving so that she doesn't wake up. This time I discover the roads northeast of Stanford University. They are named after famous universities on the East Coast: Princeton Road, Yale Road, Harvard Avenue. After half an hour of driving along the Ivy League, my granddaughter awakens and we go to the playground with grandparents and nannies from at least thirty different countries. In the past, the children's minders went to Parc Monceau in Paris, now they are here in Palo Alto. Shifts. I miss Ulrich Beck.

On Saturday mornings, I visit Kepler's. My book orders have arrived: Jonathan Galassi's *Muse* and Nicole Krauss's *Great House*. I look around the store and see about forty people in the above-sixty age group, all settled in chairs. I look for the author. But it isn't a reading session, the bookseller explains, it's "Mystery Day at Kepler's." A competition in which each person present at the bookstore reads out a short story they have written. "It's amazing," says the bookseller. The event is limited to registered participants. I withdraw with best wishes and leave the store.

Four months later, in January 2017, I'm on a plane flying over Greenland to California once again. This time I'm bringing a doll for my granddaughter. During one of our Skype conversations, I had held up two of my own dolls from the fifties for the camera and asked her: "Which doll should I bring you when I come in three weeks? Bärbel or Vroni?" My child's child decided on Vroni, short for Veronica, one with the long black hair. My father had chosen the name when he gave me the doll for Christmas in 1958. Influenced by his brief time studying at university in Munich in 1947–48, for a degree he didn't complete, my father had a penchant for FC Bayern Munich and Bavarian names. He went on to marry a woman from Gdansk. "A refugee with lung disease, and a Catholic," his mother had pointed out. But that hadn't deterred my father. He was vehemently supported by my maternal grandmother, Agnes, who saw in my father the opportunity of a lifetime for her sick daughter. She countered his mother's reservations with excellent food—duck and sausages every Sunday, for which she even haggled with the Kashubian merchant in the markets of Heidelberg. My father, a benevolent and handsome man, also a gourmand and gourmet, surrendered willingly.

The dolls had to be restored. I sought advice online: Doll Clinic Plate, Käthe-Niederkirchner-Straße in Prenzlauer Berg, Berlin. I imagined a woman from East Berlin who would look like the actress Carmen-Maja Antoni. But in the doorway stood a tall, young woman wearing an immaculate white gown that read "Doll Doctor." Gentrification, I thought. In the waiting area, I saw another woman with a very large doll. "What ails her?" I asked sympathetically.—"It's her stomach." Two weeks later, I returned to pick up the dolls. They had new fingers and hair, and the backs of their heads were mended. "Drive carefully," said Doll Doctor. I fastened the seatbelts on the dolls. Hopefully no one saw me doing this. But I was deeply happy.

Once in the Valley, I pick up on my habits. With every visit I become more confident in dealing with its inhabitants. My gaze indicates: I belong here. That is presumptuous. Because I don't. My only friend in Menlo Park, Barbara Katz Mendes, has organized a dinner for me and invited three of her girlfriends: one is thrice divorced, the other twice, the youngest is single and runs marathons. All of them teach either at Stanford or Berkeley. They are either grandmothers or have no children, and they are all vegan. They are sprightly and unapologetic. All of them have read Barbara's book *Falling in Love with Your Life*. A merry evening. I remain suspicious.

Barbara gave me a copy of her book and said, "You need to become more active, then life and love will come back." I put the book aside.

A friend and colleague of mine was delivering a lecture on Paul Celan's poem "Deathfugue" in the German Library at Stanford. I had imagined this library to be vast. But it is a rather small room that houses the collected works of German-language authors of the past fifty years. I thought I was back at Suhrkamp. I sat down next to the collected works of Heiner Müller. It was scheduled for noon, a so-called luncheon lecture. A Hispanic caterer, whose business had an Arabic name, was serving Lebanese appetizers. I thought we would eat after the lecture, but I was wrong. Everyone helped themselves beforehand and when I headed for the buffet, the lecture started and I had to sit down empty-handed. The young German historian next to me was crouching with his legs slanted to one side on a low chair; he had put so much food on his plate that on the one hand, I was worried it was going to drop on my clothes, and on the other I hoped it really would because I was hungry. I sympathized with him, though. The Valley is very expensive. My favorite supermarket is Draeger's in Menlo Park, a family business of more than ninety years. Gustave Draeger, from Szczecin, had founded it as a delicatessen in San Francisco in 1925. It stocks everything the stomach wants and has its own wine department that could give some stores in Paris a run for their money. My friend Barbara laughs about my penchant for the expensive Draeger's.

She shops at Whole Foods, which is owned by Amazon, and at Trader Joe's, which belongs to the Aldi Group.

The hotspots of the Valley—Mountain View, Palo Alto, Menlo Park—are close to the Pacific. Due to the volume of traffic and the many serpentines, however, it takes at least fifty minutes from Palo Alto to Half Moon Bay, a drawn-out coastal resort with a big marina. A friend of mine, a literary scholar and Goethe researcher, told me that she drove to Half Moon Bay twice a week to walk along the beach. She had occasionally invited me to lunch at her house in the first years of my visits. Her house is an Arcadian symbiosis of the Old and the New World. A *Bibliotheca Goethiana* amid lemon and palm trees. I believe a certain Johann Wolfgang Goethe from Frankfurt would have liked it. I imagine how much Herr Goethe would have liked to live in Palo Alto at this time. He would have been in the right spot with his genius for the interdisciplinary and his interest in political involvement.

One can walk along the beaches of Half Moon Bay for a long time and even surf in the ocean. But I can't. It's impossible to swim in northern California. The ocean is too cold, you would need a wetsuit. But that would look unflattering on me. Every now and then, I dip my toes into the water so I could at least say that my feet have touched the Pacific. When you stand on the shore of the Pacific in California, you know that on the other side of it lies China. When you stand on the east coast of Taiwan, you can imagine California. When you're in the Finistère in Brittany, you can see Martha's Vineyard south of Boston in front of your mind's eye, and vice versa. I don't have to swim in any ocean. What makes oceans special is that you can stand on the shore and imagine spaces across the vast expanse. Maybe that's what I'll do when I retire: stand by the ocean for hours and think about the other side.

Three weeks later, on the flight back to Berlin via Frankfurt am Main, I'm sitting in my window seat, Lake Tahoe underneath me, and fighting back the tears. It's easy to cry on airplanes. It's the air pressure. I decided once again to follow the example of the many couples from India. They don't cry. They fly halfway across the world to see their children and grandchildren in California, but they don't cry, at least not on the plane. Saying goodbye hurts. The countdown app is adjusted anew: at least another ninety or hundred and twenty days of digital family communication until we see each other again in person. I feel a certain sense of relief when others cry. On my return journey I was lucky. The young woman behind me was already shedding tears in the security line at San Francisco International Airport. Her boyfriend standing at the cordon, forming the shape of a heart with his fingers, only swelled the tears. By now we were above Canada and I looked at the woman sitting next to me with tears in her eyes. I peered at the screen to see if it might be the film that caused them. I saw horses and princesses. But since she was inconsolable, I asked her if I could help or comfort her somehow. She smiled and said she was crying because of the film.

On the return flights, I sometimes watch as many as four films. Afterwards I can't quite remember what those were. I admire fellow travelers who can sleep or work for hours. When the animation on the screen indicates that we are passing Greenland, I open the window-blind a tiny bit and look at the icebergs.

All that you need to survive the challenges of loving at a distance is written on the walls of the houses in Wedding, a neighborhood in northwest Berlin: MIGRATION IS NOT A CRIME.

It's 6:30 a.m. I'm on my way to the office when my GPS reroutes me to a petrol station near Müllerstraße because the one on Seestraße, which I usually use, is currently being refueled. I plan to take the reroute around Wedding only to take a picture of the grafftti on the walls.

I like Wedding. Most people in the neighborhood are foreign, just as I am in California. My friends don't understand how I can equate that. But you speak English, they say. As if that was enough. A sound command of the language is the minimum requirement for surviving in a foreign country. The entire internal navigation, or social nuance, is missing: What do people read? What do they eat? What do you see? What do you say? For instance, I don't know what my peers in California talk about. I only know what the Chinese, Hungarian, and Indian grandparents on the playgrounds in Silicon Valley don't talk about. The Valley is Babylonia. The towers are built elsewhere.

Berlin

The Havel River has always been my first choice for the letter "H" when playing City–Country–River. Decades before I had even seen the river for the first time. Unfortunately, it usually got me only five points because my fellow players would also put down the Havel in their list. There were many cities beginning with "H," but fewer rivers. Five points are unfair because the Havel is perfect, especially from Berlin-Spandau to Havelberg. After seven years of living at its banks, I know every blade of grass between Gatow and Potsdam, both from land and from the water. It is an indescribable feeling to drive a little motorboat very early on summer mornings in the middle of the capital to observe the birds and the trees. It's such a perfectly harmonious landscape that has made the uncertainties of living in Berlin easier for me. The drive between the Pfaueninsel and the banks of Kladow with the gardens of Dr. Max Fraenkel's country house to the Sacrower Lanke, where friends of mine live and where you can moor the boat, is enchanting.

In 2010, Suhrkamp Publishing House moved to Berlin. From West to East Germany. It was a smart decision. Even though I didn't want to move myself, I went along. I had imagined life in Berlin to be easier. Beyond that, I felt sorry for my hometown, Frankfurt am Main. When I was young, it was considered one of West Germany's intellectual epicenters. With the International Book Fair; the Börsenverein des Deutschen Buchhandels (Bookseller and Publishers Association); the publishing houses S. Fischer, Suhrkamp, Insel, the Jüdischer Verlag and many smaller independent enterprises; the Institute for Social Research; the Sigmund Freud Institute, and later the Fritz Bauer Institute, the city formed a focal point of philosophy, social science, Shoah research, and the book trade. And now I'm based here in the capital; it's where I entered a tattoo studio for the first time in my life, eight years after my arrival. Of course in Berlin that could have happened earlier. The boundaries of good taste are amorphous here. It is surprising how much the gap widens as soon as one leaves behind the opera houses, museums, and theaters, the experience of Berlin's everyday culture and its expression. There is a space for creation. More so than in other large cities.

After my return from California, in March 2018, I was sitting in my office alone, and the longing for my grandchildren was so painful that I thought: I would like to have them engraved on my skin. I was amused. I wondered how even these feelings create the desire for a tattoo. The longing has to burn on the skin. Apart from that, I wanted to show my grandchildren how close they are to me, that I would have them on the skin, forever. I went on the search for a suitable studio. A friend's hairdresser recommended Mirko B. in Wexstraße, who said to me after our initial consultation: "You're giving me courage to age." Now my grandchildren's initials adorn my upper arm—the design, small and classy. It didn't hurt nearly as much as I had feared. Instead, I experienced an adrenaline rush for hours afterwards and could understand why indigenous peoples perform such initiation rites.

In Berlin I often feel as foreign as I do in Menlo Park and Berkeley. Surely it's me, I absolve Berlin of any blame. I need the hills of our country's southwest, the vineyards and the proximity to France. Berlin has none of that. My friends love Berlin, including those who were born in East or West Berlin and those who moved here from other parts of the country and the world. This city attracts people who aren't deterred by its gruffness and who can make creative use of its open spaces.

Since the autumn of 2018, I have a library card issued in my name, this time in Kladow, the most southwestern part of the city. I didn't need to access a library in fifty years, since as an employee of a publishing house, I always had sufficient books to read and, in addition to that, I shopped at the local bookstore every Saturday. My library card reads: VÖBB, Verbund Öffentlicher Bibliotheken Berlins (the Public Libraries of Berlin). It is also valid in other boroughs. Considering the size of the city, that is not practical and, in

my case, is not necessary either, because I was already successful in my search for lost time. It was enough to drive from
Gatow to Kladow, park the bike and enter the library—and
there it was again: the magic of books, sorted by category. It's
that simple, I thought, just pick up old habits! Borrow a book
that you have never heard about or perhaps one that you want
to read again. I took out *4321* by Paul Auster. The atmosphere
in the three rooms of the Kladow library—the employees who
represent something timeless despite the digitized ways of bor-
rowing and returning books, the memories of Frankfurt's public libraries in the years between 1960 and 1972, both those
run by the municipality and those run by the Church—intensified the feeling that I have at concerts, at the opera, at the
theater, and in exhibitions: How much insight, innovation,
and comfort the analog culture provides. It is irreplaceable. In
all aspects and for all age groups.

San Francisco / Berkeley

I got my first-ever senior citizen ID card at the BART (Bay Area Rapid Transit) branch at the San Francisco airport in the spring of 2019. I had a little time before my return flight and was browsing the offers at the BART information booth. The lady at the counter asked me whether I was sixty-five yet. "No, not yet," I replied. "But when I come back for my granddaughter's first day of school in August, I will be," I added, pride reflecting in my voice. Following her advice, I bought a senior ticket that covers travel costs worth $24 for only $9. And proudly posted the photo of the ID card on my family and my friends' groups on WhatsApp. My friends wrote: *You are a global citizen.* I appreciate the thought. 'Global citizen'—that's what I always wanted to be, just like I always wanted to work at a publishing house. Books have allowed me to travel to many countries. My roots are in southwest Germany, in Frankfurt am Main, in Heidelberg and Mannheim, in the Taunus, in the Rheingau, and Hofheim-Wildsachsen. When

I sit on the bench next to my husband's grave in the Wildsachsen neighborhood of Hofheim, I grow so many roots that I am unable to get back up. The roots reach far into the earth. I often enjoy sitting there, and feeling the roots within. I didn't grow old with my husband. But I aged with Michael Douglas. He is not aware of me, though. After I finished watching all three seasons of *The Kominsky Method* recently, I remembered that I used to watch *The Streets of San Francisco* regularly from 1974 to 1977. A strange familiarity with Michael Douglas sets in, retrospectively, so to speak. I used to watch the show based in the city on the West Coast fifty years ago, but had never been to the US. But now I know San Francisco by heart. On one of my first visits, coming in on the Caltrain from Menlo Park, I had taken a bicycle with me. No sooner had I left the station than I realized that it was more or less impossible to ride on most of the streets. Especially down the streets. They are much too steep. But I can ride as far as the Pacific, westward along Market Street, via Fell Street, or Fulton Street, straight ahead, without any major inclines through Golden Gate Park. Once you're there, you can see the Golden Gate Bridge and Presidio Park in the northeast, the boroughs of Mission and Castro in the southeast. The Golden Gate Bridge is only beautiful from afar, but up close it is feels rather eerie.

Once I took the bus back to the Caltrain station from Presidio Park, and had to mount my bike onto the rack at the front of the bus by myself. It took me almost eight embarrassing minutes and the bus driver and the passengers kindly waited. In Europe, they would have started shouting by then, but the Americans are by far the most patient people I have ever met. It was just as embarrassing when older, much fitter, cyclists overtook me at the Golden Gate Park while calling out, amicably but firmly: "Bike on your left!" Weeks later, I exacted my revenge when I rode past a group of tourists on bikes in the park, along the large bison enclosure—perhaps from Germany?—and zealously rang my bell as I yelled, "Bike on your left!" The airs of assimilation.

On a walk through Buena Vista Park, I suddenly remembered my classmate Paul who had said to me: "After we graduate, we'll move to San Francisco." We were both fourteen and I was delighted at the thought but had other plans for myself. After graduation, I moved to France. But Paul came to San Francisco, studied mathematics, and lived in a Zen monastery, where he met his wife. The two of them now live in the Netherlands, and their sons are based in New York. Somehow, I feel like other people are better than me at leaving their home countries and living in a foreign land. Twelve years ago, out of the blue, Paul showed up in front of the Suhrkamp stand at the Frankfurt Book Fair and asked for me. We had a nice chat. Nothing had changed between us. He was always creative and open to change, I was not. It felt as though it was 1968 again and we were sitting in the bus after school. He talked about all the things that were possible and I liked to believe him, but none of it applied to me.

San Francisco is considered the city with the biggest gap between rich and poor in the US. Even a regular flaneur can see that. Houses that can be bought for thirty million dollars are advertised with the tagline "Versace meets Versailles." While a block away, some ten thousand homeless people are living in tents. The local residents keep the homeless away from the streets by putting large plants in snazzy pots on the sidewalks. The homeless keep moving away from the city. Even though the Silicon Valley continuously encroaches on the Silicon City because the forests to the south and north of the Bay Area are frequently ravaged by wildfires. The Pioneer Monument on Fulton Street feels more topical than ever. The city keeps reinventing itself—from the gold rush to building the railway, to artificial intelligence and to whatever else is yet to come.

Once their decision to move from Menlo Park to Berkeley was finalized, the children took me along to one of the open houses. That's the American way of buying and selling property. The houses that are for sale are emptied, refurbished, and presented by the estate agents, aiming to entice the respective target group. After seeing the third house, my granddaughter and I stayed back on a playground in Piedmont surrounded by redwoods and we sang together: *Was müssen das für Bäume sein, wo die großen Elefanten spazieren gehen, ohne sich zu stoßen?—What kind of trees would those have to be where the big elephants go walking without bumping their heads?* Earlier, one of the agents had noticed my German accent and approached me. His father had been born in Frankfurt am Main and managed to flee to California as a teenager along with his parents in 1933. Herr Rosenzweig talked about Frankfurt as though he knew every street, even though he had only been to the city once following an invitation by the Department for Urban Culture. His father, however, had talked about Frankfurt every day, he said. He had never truly arrived in California nor returned to Germany. This makes me think of my Israeli friend and colleague Uri Lev. His father too didn't feel comfortable in his place of refuge in Haifa. He talked about Lviv all day long. His son, tired of the constant lamentations, left the family at age fourteen to live in Kibbutz Mizra. He later married the granddaughter of the founder of the kibbutz. Today, Uri and Ruth have four children and ten grandchildren and all of them live in the kibbutz. How much I envy them. The kibbutz is definitely *the* model to avoid loving at a distance.

My mother and my aunt talked about Gdansk all day every day, about their childhood in Schönbeck, their parents' general store and the inn in winters, going to church in the next village and their years at the Ursulines' boarding school in Gdansk. They adamantly refused to return ever since their escape in 1946. All efforts by their husbands and their daughter and niece failed. A boat trip from Lübeck to Gdansk, which my father had thought up as a surprise, and had already made reservations for, had to be canceled. About six months before they died, both of them claimed that now was the right time to return to their homeland, even though neither of them was in any shape to undertake such a journey. I had taken both my aunt and my mother, from Mannheim and Kronberg am Taunus, to the capital during my Berlin decade so that I could care for them myself. My aunt died a chain smoker, peacefully at eighty-four at Fasanenplatz in Berlin. My mother behaved wisely and asked for a burial at the Baltic Sea—that was her plan to finally return to Gdansk. She spen the last six months of her life with me in Berlin-Gatow with a historical map of Gdansk that I had bought at Düssel, from the antiquarian books and art store on Gendarmenmarkt.

I'm not just a member of the public library in Kladow but also, together with my grandchildren, of the Contra Costa County Public Library on the hill above Berkeley next to Tilden Regional Park. The children can play there, paint and read, or be read to. Everyone who is able to write their name on their own, and without help, can become a member. That's another thing to live for: accompanying my grandchildren to concerts and public libraries. I take out the recently published second volume of Sylvia Plath's letters from 1956 to 1963, a monumental edition with a moving introduction by her daughter Frieda Hughes.

On weekdays, the nearby restaurant Kensington Inn, located in the hills between Berkeley Hills and Tilden Regional Park, is crowded with elderly people who finish their walks by 10 a.m. There are sixteen variations of eggs for breakfast. My favorite is the Firenza omelette stuffed with spinach and mushrooms. A lovely gentleman approaches and asks, "Is your name Cindy?"—"Unfortunately, no," I reply. And draw a deep breath, telling him that my father used to call me Cindy when I was a little girl and sang to me the song "Cindy, oh Cindy," but the gentleman had already made an excuse and moved on. My father sang both Eddy Fisher's English version from 1956 and Margot Eskens' German version. The text of the German cover is a little different, because in that version poor Cindy is left by a man. Eddy Fisher, on the other hand, asks his Cindy to remain faithful to him while he serves in the navy. The gentleman has left by now. There is something tragic about his Cindy, it's not me, but it isn't anyone else either. I turn my attention back to my omelette and the online edition of the *Süddeutsche Zeitung* from the following day, because of the nine-hour time difference it's accessible at breakfast time instead of in the evening. Just as *Heute Journal* and the news afterwards. Everything happens in the mornings. That is the best thing about the time difference, the fact that all the information of the following day is already available in the mornings, and on Saturdays there is a special section on the Bundesliga soccer matches.

The children's first-ever day of school, which is increasingly becoming a big family celebration in Germany as it was customary in the former German Democratic Republic, is an unspectacular event in the US. Which is surprising because children's birthdays and other holidays are celebrated quite extravagantly. In the schoolyard of the Berkeley Arts Magnet School, parents take a couple of photos; few grandparents are present. My eldest granddaughter has now officially started school and, reassured by another advent of education in the family, I fly back to Germany and to my last seventy-five days at Suhrkamp. My fortieth Frankfurt Book Fair is approaching.

In the early 1960s, my mother had sometimes rented out my childhood bedroom to visitors; breakfast was included. People from faraway countries came for the spring and autumn fairs and for the motor show. Once, a visitor from India put a round basket in the room. My mother and I were very scared that a snake might escape from the basket. And then, at some point, came Frau Hanske from Lübeck, who unfortunately struck up a friendship with my mother and from then on occupied my bedroom twice a year until she sold her business of selling fabrics and ceramics from Scandinavia. Each time, she would bring me a dress from a Finnish manufacturer. I would only wear it on the days that she was around because no one in Frankfurt wore such dresses and certainly no one in my neighborhood.

I visited Frankfurt Book Fair for the first time as a student in 1970. From 1973, the dates of the Fair usually coincided with the beginning of the semester. On the last day of the Fair, we, students of Romance philology, would rush to the stands of the French, Spanish, and Italian publishers to grab a few bargains. From 1980 to 2019, I was on the "right" side wearing an exhibitor's pass. I never missed a Fair in all these years. As a rights manager, it was *the* event of the year for me. The entire guild would come together—just like in Antiquity or in the Middle Ages. You would meet most of your colleagues from abroad just once a year—to me, this was always the best part of my job. And this didn't change in times of digital communication. You have to see one another, you just have to see the other person, and not just on a screen—this holds true for grandchildren as well as for colleagues from a hundred and seventy countries.

*Working
at a Distance*

Working at a Distance

There are sociological treatises on migration and on tourism. But I'm not aware of any noteworthy scientific publications on the nature of business travel. I would like to know more about it, read more about how the perception of distance changes with respect to traveling privately and for business. Therefore, I differentiate between the four kinds of travel that I have experienced and are incommensurable to one another: travels to be with family living abroad, to explore another country, traveling for business, or for leisure. I never understood traveling to another country for the sole purpose of relaxation. Which is why I was grateful for always having a reason to travel. Moreover, my job can be summarized as "disseminating knowledge from literature and science into the global market." As a young employee at a publishing house, I conducted my first sale of translation rights—or the right to translate a book originally written in the German into a foreign language and publish the volume—to the French publisher

Gallimard in 1980. The book was *Preussische Profile* by journalists Sebastian Haffner and Wolfgang Venohr, which had been published in the nonfiction program of Athenäum Verlag in Königstein im Taunus. The fact that this important book, which went on to become a bestseller, was published in my first week of joining Athenäum after graduating university was typical beginner's luck. My contract of employment was for a job in the rights and press-and-publicity departments. On my first day, the publisher put an electric typewriter and two index-card boxes on my desk. One was almost twice as long as the other; it contained addresses of newspapers and broadcasting companies in Germany along with the respective contact persons who were supposed to receive review copies. It had names like Rudolf Augstein, Marcel Reich-Ranicki, Fritz Raddatz, and Joachim Kaiser. The smaller box held names of foreign publishers who were supposed to receive books for review and possible translation into various languages. I was delighted to discover the names of the French and Italian publishing houses that brought out works of the authors I had studied at university: Gallimard; Grasset; Seuil; Feltrinelli; Einaudi; Mondadori. But on the cards were also handwritten addresses and contact persons of the famous New York–based publishers: Farrar, Straus & Giroux; Alfred Knopf; Harcourt Brace Jovanovich; and Pantheon. They were the American publishers of Thomas Mann, Bertolt Brecht, Anna Seghers, and Hermann Hesse. I had just turned twenty-six and thought, now I can write to the editors who work at those renowned houses and offer them books for translation into French or

Italian or English! And it reaffirmed that this is what I wanted
to do for the rest of my life.

I had told my classmates at the Frankfurt-Bornheim elemen-
tary school that I was going to be a writer only to out myself
as an employee in the publishing industry one year later, in
third grade. The teacher had explained that writer Astrid
Lindgren would take her manuscript to a house—she did not
mention the word "publisher," let alone the name Rabén &
Sjögren—and that there were people at that house who helped
her turn that manuscript into a book. That was it! That was
what I wanted to do. I ran home and told my mother that I
wanted to become a person who helps Astrid Lindgren make
a book. With her very own blend of interest in her only child
and total incomprehension of her manic reading, my mother
confirmed: "Yes, that's what you shall do." And with that the
question was resolved once and for all. I never thought of
becoming a writer again. Helping writers publish their works,
that was the most exciting thing I had ever heard of. I realized
this in third grade.

Since my success wasn't limited to the authors Haffner and
Venohr and I was able to conclude numerous other contracts
with foreign publishers at the 1980 Frankfurt Book Fair,

Athenäum relented and expanded the rights department to include the drafting of contracts for authors, translators, and editors. They sent me on a training course on copyright law and liberated me from the unloved work in the press-and-publicity department. This also happened for reasons of self-preservation, since I had mailed the German translation of African author Nuruddin Farah's debut novel, *Sweet and Sour Milk,* to all media outlets in the country, with the result that every literary supplement had printed a short review or at least mentioned the title. The publisher had to bring out a second edition immediately after the book's initial publication, even before the bookstores had sold a single copy. The first print-run was of 300 copies and the newbie had mailed 150 review copies. No one had told me how many copies the first edition comprised or explained that only a certain percentage of the printed stock could be sent out for reviews.

I was much relieved to lose the press-and-publicity profile. It was extremely tedious. You would talk to a journalist about the respective catalog for about sixty minutes and in the end you might still get bad reviews. You don't have any influence over it. But things are different in the rights department. The translation is made on the basis of a contract that governs the royalties and conditions of the license. A license can be for a translation into another language, a film adaptation, a different print edition or an audio book. In 1980, we had no inkling of licenses into digital formats. The allure of this craft that is dedicated to the worldwide dissemination of literature has drawn me throughout the forty years of my career. Most people don't know much about publishing rights and licensing, but it can have a great effect on global book trade. All you need is a text and you can sell licenses for translations into one hundred languages, for various film, theater, and game formats. A good example to demonstrate the market power of licenses is J. K. Rowling's *Harry Potter* series. But that didn't yet exist when I started out. What has always fascinated me about working with rights and licenses is the strategic task involved in it. There is content that is only relevant for a certain period of time and there are topics and motifs within literature and the humanities that are timeless. Serving those works and placing them in such a way that they are available in the short or long term, depending on the content—I felt distinguished to be able to practice this special craft. France was, due to my university studies and my very early love for our neighboring country, my favorite market.

Gerhard Kemper, Romance philologist and study counselor at the Heinrich von Gagern Grammar School in Frankfurt—who advised the students to eat, as he did, like an Englishman in the mornings, like a German at lunchtime, and like a Frenchman in the evenings—stood in front of the class and prepared us for an exchange program in the twin city of Lyon. We were supposed to attend school in France for six weeks: for the boys, it would be the classical grammar school; for the girls, the Sisters of Sainte Geneviève in the old city. Dr. Kemper had explained that schools in Lyon were different from ours. In 1969, some of the former Nazis were sent into early retirement and new teachers from universities were recruited; they introduced varied subjects in the curriculum such as "sexuality and aggression" and "capitalism and subjugation." There were constant discussions—the study groups outnumbered the students. It wasn't the same in France, despite the '68 movement, Dr. Kemper explained. He expected the students of his French class to adapt to local customs. From the code of conduct at the schools he segued to the host families. "No matter what they say about the Germans in the families—you shall remain polite." I was excited. I wanted to go to France because I liked their language and because I wanted to make peace. My parents had only ever traveled through France to holiday at the Costa Brava. Each time I asked why we weren't staying over—the Camargue, Sète, Perpignan were beautiful—but my parents didn't know a word of French and so we always drove past, first in our Beetle, then in the VW 1500/1600, en route to Spain.

This was the first time I would visit France on my own, without my parents. I saw myself an ambassador of our country. I wanted to be diplomatic yet amenable. Dr. Kemper had described in detail the crimes committed by the Germans in France. I admired him for his stance. He did not accept the objection some students voiced because we had already talked about the Nazi crimes, the Shoah and the Second World War in our history class. Dr. Kemper believed that history lessons alone would not help prepare the students for meeting the host families, and therefore his instructions were required. It was a matter of great honor that the French families were willing to take us in, that too for six weeks no less, and who, beyond that, were determined to send their own children to live with German families in the summer of the same school year. The students needn't be afraid, the host families would surely be friendly but the possibility that our presence might wake traumatic memories in older French people could not be ruled out—our history lessons could not prepare us for that. I found this moving, and departed Germany determined to please the French and to explain, as much as my language skills would allow, that our generation was going to ensure that there would never be another war or another Auschwitz.

The host families and exchange students were standing at Lyon train station with placards in their hands. My partner student was called Lucette and she came from a family of farmers and vintners in the Beaujolais. Her mother was a widow with three children. Lucette's father had died in a tractor accident when her mother was pregnant with their third child. At the time, Madame Margand was just twenty-four years old. The teachers in charge of the exchange program had allocated the participants according to their social class. The children of Frankfurt's bank directors were paired with the children of Lyon's bank directors; the children of doctors, lawyers, and teachers were also sent to live with their counterparts. After working for the automobile club, my father had become the director of Frankfurt's fur fair and of the Fur

Traders Association. There was no such thing in Lyon. So the only remaining option was the widow in the Beaujolais.

I couldn't sleep at all on the first night at the farmhouse. As an only child, I wasn't used to sharing a room with others. I didn't understand a word that my host or Lucette spoke. Both seemed lovely and their language was melodious. The "diplomatic mission" for which I had come receded into the distance and I was disheartened. Besides, there was no telephone at the farm. Ten goats, twelve cows, one pig, chickens, cats, and a black Labrador called Mirette. On the evening of my arrival, I had been taken around the wine cellar and the fromagerie, where the home-made chèvres in various stages of maturity were stored. I had written to my parents informing them of my safe arrival. The postman was supposed to collect the letter next afternoon.

"Bonjour ma petite," sang Madame Margand the next morning across the large kitchen where all her children were sitting: Lucette, Mireille, Jerôme. "You can help me pick beans." I wasn't prepared for a farm-stay vocabulary and had to constantly look up the words in the dictionary. I was embarrassed because I was boastful of the third-best result in the preparatory test for the exchange program. We had read the annotated students' edition of Camus's The Stranger, and closely followed everything that had happened in Paris in 1968, but no one in the Beaujolais was interested in any of that. Lucette had read Camus in school, too, but she hadn't enjoyed it. Mireille and Jerôme were attending vocational school for agriculture and didn't even know of Camus. Marie

Margand had attended school until she was fourteen. She knew neither Camus nor Sartre nor Simone de Beauvoir.

I tried to keep my composure. Whatever Dr. Kemper had taught us all about France did not apply in the Beaujolais. The family knew little about Germany too and they didn't talk about the war and the Nazis. Lucette's grandfather, the target group of my diplomatic offensive, told me how he had helped a German soldier who wanted to desert. Or something like that. Because even though I got better at my comprehension skills with every passing day, I was nowhere near fluent. The French language that I was trying to learn remained music to my ears and the recurring songs on the radio by Julien Clerc, Jean-Jacques Goldman, Johnny Halliday, and Georges Moustaki reinforced this. The conversations in the Margand family revolved around the approaching grape harvest, the chèvre, the neighbors, the countless relatives, weddings, and births. I learnt how to make mayonnaise, how to add lemon and a touch of butter to the green beans. After a week, I was responsible for making the soup for supper and I would add the vinaigrette of mustard and mayonnaise to the lettuce. After three weeks, I knew the names of Madame Margand's thirteen siblings and their children, which earned me the entire family's goodwill. In the evenings, the five of us sat at the long farmhouse table to watch war films on TV in which perfidious and wicked "Boches" tortured French people. None of those present made a connection between the Nazis and the German soldiers and me. But I did—I deferred my diplomatic mission until later.

I returned every summer to the Beaujolais. Diplomacy, luckily, was successfully conducted on the political stage. I was content with that and much relieved. Lucette and I became close friends. We took turns visiting each other, but I went to the Beaujolais more often than Lucette came to Frankfurt. France was just more beautiful. And apart from that, Lucette became a wine expert and had engagements. I paid attention to the structural changes in France, where wines were hyped by the Nouvelle Cuisine and the Beaujolais Nouveau in the 1960s and especially the 1970s only to disappear into regional insignificance at the beginning of the 2000s. Almost all of Lucette's relatives changed their profession: from being vintners, they chose social careers such as logistics and tourism. Nowadays, they only produce small amounts for the respective local wine cooperative.

The 1980 Frankfurt Book Fair wasn't truly international. It only seemed like that to us; none of us foresaw the globalization that would set in ten years later. Asia, with the exception of Japan, wasn't participating in the rights trade and neither were the Arab nations. In the 1980s, the international copyright conventions, the legal basis for the rights trade, had not yet been ratified by all countries. Ten years later, when I was responsible for the rights and licenses department at Luchterhand Publishing House and worked closely with Günter Grass, Peter Bichsel, Peter Härtling, Ernst Jandl and, 1991 onward, Christa Wolf, the situation had changed dramatically. The fall of the Berlin Wall led to an expansion into other European languages for the works of German literature and science. In the 1990s publishers in the Czech Republic, Poland, Hungary, Bulgaria, Romania, and the Baltic countries founded private and independent publishing houses. They came to the Frankfurt and London Book Fairs to buy translation rights. What extraordinary opportunities arose for the British, French, German, Spanish, Italian and Scandinavian publishers! Opening up possibilities for a lively multilateral trade beyond borders. Every newly established publishing house in Central and Eastern Europe opened up access to new readers for all the other European authors. After the Balkan Wars, by 1999, Slovenia, Croatia, Serbia, and Bosnia had entered the stage. Bit by bit, new members joined the Universal Copyright Convention: apart from numerous Arab and African countries, from Asia emerged China and Korea, which completely restructured the global market. The worldwide trade with literature, nonfiction, academic nonfiction, children's books, content for theater and films had begun—one could sign contracts with publishers from across the globe. The already dominant English-language authors from all five continents continued their triumph on the international bestseller lists, followed by works in Spanish. For all other European literatures, it was important to develop systems of dissemination and networks to find markets for their authors who were writing in their own languages.

I joined Suhrkamp Publishing House on February 1, 1995. On November 8, 1994, I had signed the employment contract with them and quit Luchterhand. My primary responsibility at Suhrkamp was to manage translation rights and licenses. The publishing house was founded by Peter Suhrkamp on July 1, 1950, and Helene Ritzerfeld had been there from the very beginning. She established the rights and licenses department and headed it ever since. Dr. Siegfried Unseld, then publisher at Suhrkamp, introduced me to Frau Ritzerfeld on September 19, 1994. Our age difference amounted to forty years exactly. I was forty, Frau Ritzerfeld was eighty. She worked and lived on the third floor of the publishing house. Her reputation was legendary—and with good reason. She ruled over the inventory of authors' rights and wanted to share neither her knowledge nor the task. But since the market was expanding, becoming more global, she could no longer make do without help. That was not her view but that of Dr. Unseld. I understood her reluctance. I wouldn't have much liked to share such an empire either. Frau Ritzerfeld was happiest when I left the office every day at 4 p.m. on the dot. She would continue working till later without the disruption and presence of a potential successor. She always waved at me affably at the end of the day and was a little disappointed when I arrived on time the next morning, sharp at 7:45 a.m., to greet her cordially in return: "Good morning, Frau Ritzerfeld." She would arrive at 7:30 a.m. every day. Nothing ever changed about this ritual during the five years that we were fortunate enough to spend together.

Helene Ritzerfeld sat at Peter Suhrkamp's desk, a pencil, a fountain pen, a notepad, and a dictaphone next to her. She dictated three tapes per day: letters to the authors, contract negotiations, rejections of unreasonable inquiries for licenses. With her pen she added the following information to a cover sheet to make the work of the colleagues in the transcription department easier. The addressee in one column, the length of the dictated letter in the other: Heiner Hesse, 1–25; Giorgio Strehler, 25–34; Stephen Joyce, 35–42; Hans Magnus Enzensberger, 43–63. The shelves behind her desk held all the translations of the works by Bertolt Brecht, Hermann Hesse, and Max Frisch. Those three authors ranked without competition, independent of the alphabetical order. The shelves opposite her desk were arranged in perfect order: Theodor W. Adorno . . . Jurek Becker . . . Thomas Bernhard. She would put the translations of works by authors worthy of the honor of standing in Frau Ritzerfeld's office on the shelf herself. My colleague Claudia Brandes and I were allowed to arrange the other complimentary copies which were housed in the room next door, beginning with the letter "C" on the shelves. We were not allowed to enter anything into the database she had created: RITZ1. That was her prerogative. The Windows DOS database application Open Access 4—OA4 for short—outdated by the time, wasn't particularly user-friendly, but it allowed us to create data sets with connections to other spreadsheets within the company with comparatively little effort. The spreadsheet titled "RITZ1"—with the columns listing country, licensee, title, date of agreement, term, advance, and royalties—was used to keep track of the translation agreements. When Frau Ritzerfeld developed the first databases for the rights and licenses department at Suhrkamp, she was already in her eighties. The fact that she gave this file a personalized name, RITZ1, bespeaks great confidence and even predicted the developments in Silicon Valley. Helene Ritzerfeld was a virtuosa: she strolled through the works of Brecht, Habermas, Hesse, Frisch, Johnson, and Koeppen like Vladimir Horowitz through Scarlatti's piano sonatas. She once developed a complete and bestselling program of Hesse's works in half an hour for a South Korean publisher. Those were the twilight years of the analog age. We suspected it but couldn't quite picture the radical changes to the work processes yet.

The 1995 Frankfurt Book Fair was my first with Suhrkamp. Turin-based publisher Giuglio Einaudi met Marcel Beyer, whose work, *The Karnau Tapes,* he wanted to publish in Italian. I had finally arrived at the center of the literary scene—where I had always wanted to, ever since my first encounter with books—representing one of the best publishing houses in the world that provided the foundation for successful trade with its authors' works. The reception for the foreign publishers and agents at the house of Siegfried and Ulla Unseld, which took place on the Saturday morning of the Fair, was the absolute highlight of my professional career to that date. The event had been hosted by Dr. Unseld since the 1960s, modeled after the reception for the literary critics which was held for the first time in 1959. The invitation to the 1995 reception was signed with the names of Siegfried Unseld, Helene Ritzerfeld, and my own—I almost fainted when I saw my name. Luckily, Frau Ritzerfeld had told me before the Fair how horrified she had been when an employee of the publishing house, for whom she had had some hope, if only a little, once took one of the canapés that were served at the reception and was forced to answer a question by the British sociologist and science publisher John Thompson with a mouthful of food. I was immensely grateful to Frau Ritzerfeld for mentioning this inexcusable faux pas. After the Fair, I was back at Suhrkamp on Lindenstraße in Frankfurt am Main. My office was diagonally across from Frau Ritzerfeld's and looked out onto the courtyard. When Dr. Unseld's blue Jaguar turned onto the parking lot in the mornings, I felt safe.

Roughly one year later, on August 23, 1996, my husband's work *Die Geschichte der italienischen Literatur* (The History of Italian Literature) was published. The book-launch event was held on September 26 in the presence of Italian authors Luigi Malerba and Paola Capriolo as well as the literary scholars Maria Gazetti and Wolf Dieter Lange. Publisher Inge Feltrinelli made a positive statement on my husband's literary work.

Those were the best summers of my life—both professionally and personally speaking. Until my husband died in a car accident in 2001. How could I go on without him? I used to wonder. Of course you could go on living in the trees, like the baron in the Italo Calvino novel. You could go on living with the books. The text and the manifold ways of its reception, its use, its exploitation, the literary as well as the scientific work. A cosmos in which we were once together as one—inseparable from each other. Ever since then, I have been living alone with all the books and working on their dissemination; reading and organizing them, frequenting libraries, as well as reading out loud to my grandchildren.

The globalization of the publishing market resulted in the establishment of book fairs in countries outside of Europe. German publishers and editors became esteemed partners and were frequently invited. A great deal of travel began that took me to the new markets in East Asia, the Middle East, India, Russia, and Brazil. I can't compare trade in books with that of other products—like water pumps, chinaware, clothes, for example. But I was always under the impression that the content business—whether literary or trade fiction, crime novels, children's books, or works of nonfiction, or cookbooks— creates a special kind of closeness between the business partners irrespective of differences in culture. A book is a mirror of its society. Publishing houses that are willing to pay the costs of translations are not only going to pay attention to sales potential and expected profits alone but also to the social relevance of the text by an author from a different country that they choose to include in their publishing program. It may bring in profits and recognition if an author makes it to a bestseller list, wins an important literary prize, or is awarded the Nobel Prize.

The days spent in travel are filled with appointments. One is spared the sightseeing. Instead of the obligatory sights, I chose to visit bookstores and publishing houses wherever possible. In countries where I couldn't read the language, I went to the bookstores accompanied by colleagues or translators. In the analog age, I took notes with a pen and a pad, listing out translations from the German-language world that lined the shelves. After the turn of the century, phone cameras proved even more helpful. I was satisfied with the array of German-language literature translated into the respective national language in the bookstores of Paris, Madrid, Rome, Amsterdam, Prague, Budapest, Ljubljana, and Copenhagen. I experienced my Waterloo not on a business trip but as a grandmother at Kepler's bookstore in Menlo Park decades later in 2016. There was only one copy of the English edition of a work by a German author in the large bookstore in one of the richest parts of the world and that too in the profitable pre-Christmas period: Bertolt Brecht's *Love Poems*, published in 2014 by Liveright in the fantastic translation by Tom Kuhn and David Constantine. That was merely a tiny sliver of Europe in Silicon Valley.

Business travel never exhausted me. On the contrary, I felt like I understood more of a country's society than I did on any touristic travel. Whenever I sat in the playgrounds in the Valley or elsewhere in the Bay Area during the second decade of the twenty-first century, I missed the familiar comfort and the socially relevant compass of business trips. You have a business card that proves your expertise. Should I get a business card that reads "Grandmother"? Grandmother in two continents. That's not a unique selling point.

Kolkata

On one of the many transatlantic flights, I read the article titled "The Planet Fights Back" by David Wallace-Wells in *New York Magazine*. It says that cities like Kolkata are going to become uninhabitable within the next fifty years. That would surely be a catastrophe because it is a lovely city. When we were children, we sang "Kalkutta liegt am Ganges" by Vico Torriani, a song about his love for a woman named Madeleine and about many rivers, the Ganges, the Nile, and the Congo being the ones outside of Europe. Between 2008 and 2017, I visited Calcutta—officially known by its Bengali name "Kolkata" since 2001—four times for business. My first impression corresponded to my longing and the resulting expectations. You either flee or you fall in love with the city. I fell in love. I learnt that Kolkata is located not on banks of the Ganges but of the Hooghly River, the eastern distributary of the Ganges in the state of West Bengal, India. This confused me. If you had assumed that Kolkata was on the banks of the

Ganges for nearly fifty years only to learn that it is on the Hooghly—which sounds very Swiss but is hard to pronounce both in German and in English—you would find yourself disappointed.

During the 2007 Fair, at the Suhrkamp office in Frankfurt, my colleague Ulrich Breth and I met the Kolkata-based publisher Naveen Kishore, who was planning a literary series of books by German-language authors for his publishing house, Seagull Books. To that end, he intended to buy translation rights from Suhrkamp. We assumed he meant translation rights for the Hindi and Bengali languages; instead, he wanted world rights for the English language. This was in direct competition with the publishing houses in New York and London and did not initially attract our attention—until Naveen invited us to visit Kolkata to understand his proposition better and assess the situation for ourselves. We flew to Kolkata via Delhi and landed at thirty minutes past midnight. Naveen picked us up in his car. That first drive from the airport to the hotel has since become one of the iconic moments of my life. It is the space between what you expect and what you see and experience. That's the true nature of traveling and that's why it is so valuable.

In 2008, many of the Kolkata's poor lived on the streets. This situation has changed a lot over the past decade. Sometimes I think that in Kolkata people move from the streets and into houses, while in San Francisco they move out of the houses and onto the streets. The bustle of the Bengali metropolis with its overcrowded buses, throngs of people on the streets, open roadside kitchens, and the thousand different kinds of smell contrasts with the calm found elsewhere in the city: the house of the great Bengali poet, painter, and composer Rabindranath Tagore, who was also the first Asian to receive the Nobel Prize in Literature; the Botanical Garden along the Hooghly; and the park surrounding the Victoria Memorial. Time passes more slowly in these places, and you can immerse yourself in the interplay between light and shadow in the warmth of January.

The purpose of this first visit to Kolkata and Delhi was for us get to know the market and to plan of a series of books translated from the German, which subsequently established a collaboration between Seagull Books, the Goethe-Institut, and Suhrkamp. Later, other German-language publishers would join us. The Indian book market is unique; it comprises not only the dominant English-language trade pulishers established by the British and American media conglomerates but also many small, independent enterprises, and regional-language presses, catering to a vast readership across 120 different languages. Yet there are only a handful of translators for Hindi, Bengali, Tamil, Malayalam—languages that have the potential to connect millions of readers—who are able to translate from German. Hermann Hesse's novel *Siddhartha* is one of the few works that have been translated into more than ten Indian languages. Interestingly, there are a few international-style chain bookstores in Kolkata; besides these, bookselling mainly happens through streetside stalls, small independent stores, and at College Street, the university neighborhood in the north of the city. I bought a book with a likeness of Thomas Mann on its cover. From the copyright I learnt that this was a Bengali translation of *Tonio Kröger* and other early stories. The book stalls are lined up along the university buildings like the stalls of the Parisian bouquinistes along the Seine. Translator Subroto Saha walked me to the famous Indian Coffee House, which has played host to at least as many authors and philosophers as the Café de Flore and the Deux-Magots in Paris. Aside from the predictable dominance of the colonial British when it comes to architecture, garden design, club life, and sports, I am surprised by the diversity of similarities between Kolkata and Paris.

A friend who teaches at the Indian Institute of Management in Kolkata invited me to dine at the elegant Bengal Club, which in the past solely allowed membership to men. Women were permitted only when accompanied by men. Founded in 1827, the Bengal Club only began admitting Indian citizens as members in 1959. We sat in the club and talked about the generational arc. Varun regularly travels from Kolkata to Hyderabad, where his mother lives. He has worked out a system with his siblings whereby they take turns caring for their mother. From Hyderabad he flies to Delhi, where his wife, originally from Kolkata, waits for him. They look after their grandchildren when the sons and daughters are at work. Like many of the friends my age, I too live in-between the generations. The multigenerational house of my great-grandparents stood in Wiesloch in Northern Baden; mine now floats between Berlin and San Francisco. A cloud in which we love.

Four years later, in 2012, publisher Naveen Kishore founded the Seagull School of Publishing. Twice a year, about fifty students receive training in editing, production, and sales and marketing over the course of three months. Publishing professionals from across the world are invited as guest lecturers. I flew out at the beginning of July, an unfortunate time in terms of weather, for my first lecture. As I sat at the Heineken Bar in transit at the Abu Dhabi airport, I thought: Why are you doing this to yourself? Surely there is someone in India who can explain contract negotiation and selling licenses to the students. By then it was too late, I was sitting at the bar at the airport, waiting for my connecting flight to Kolkata along with itinerant and migrant laborers and a few tourists, drinking a large beer in a country where the locals don't drink alcohol.

After I landed in Kolkata, the driver took me to the Tollygunge Club, where I would stay. Created by the British as a facility for equestrian sport in 1895, the club is situated in a large, quaint park in South Kolkata. I welcomed the relative freshness. The next morning, I was woken up at 4 a.m. by the shouting in the park. A golf tournament had begun early in the morning. I watched with interest, even though I don't know anything about golf. But the dry greens, the nocturnal hour, the men dressed in white, the rising sun, the jackal at the edge of the park, the first sounds from the hotel kitchen made me feel cheery and confident that my journey was worthwhile. This impression strengthened five hours later at the school: the students were mainly women, some of whom wanted to start their own publishing ventures. I gave my everything to nurture this dream. "What ideal conditions for publishing you have," I said to the listeners. "You have a huge market for print and digital productions! And you can work in at least two languages—English and one of the many Indian languages." Together we imagined how the young publishers would negotiate licenses in the global market. How they would turn their own contents into books and e-books, and sell rights to film-production companies and streaming services. Nothing seemed impossible during those two days and all my doubts had dissipated.

My last night in Kolkata was July 14, Bastille Day. I learned that it was celebrated at the French consulate in Kolkata. And gratefully accepted Naveen's invitation to accompany him to the event. I recalled the Bastille Day receptions at the French embassy in Berlin and at the consulate in Frankfurt am Main. In both cities I had had the home-turf advantage with regard to the bilateral relations between France and Germany. I had sung the "Marseillaise," the German national anthem and the European anthem with confidence along with the other guests in Berlin. But here I didn't know a single line of the Indian national anthem. There were quite a few speeches made on the occasion and Bengali music played. It took a long time until the delicious buffet was finally opened to us. I had taken up a strategic position close to the buffet laden with Bengali delicacies. Since the room was vast and we were standing close to one another, I had failed to notice the other tables offering a plethora of French cheeses.

The worry that I wouldn't be able to put enough on my plate was unfounded, since all the Bengali guests pounced on the Camembert, the goat's cheese, the Gruyère, and the other twenty varieties that had been flown in from Paris with no expense spared. A cheese frenzy on July 14. An exception, a feast for the palate, because most supermarkets in Kolkata don't stock cheese from France. The guests with whom I had ended up at a table looked at my lentils and my chicken with pity. They couldn't understand why I hadn't taken any cheese and even asked, with sympathy, if I was lactose intolerant.

It was, and will be, my only Bastille Day in India—it is unbearably hot in summer. On the flight back to Europe, this time via Delhi, I looked out of the airplane window about forty minutes after take-off from Kolkata. I couldn't believe my eyes when I saw the snow-covered peaks peeping through the clouds. I had to look up at the mountain ranges, not gaze downwards like we do when flying over the Alps. I sat there, in awe, and whispered to my neighbor, "Is that the Himalayas?" He looked up from his laptop briefly, a little irritated, "Of course." I pressed my face to the window for the next thirty minutes. I had never seen anything so moving.

In March 2017, I returned to the Seagull School of Publishing for the last time. I no longer questioned the long flight. In my mind's eye, I envisioned several generations of publishers dedicating their lives to literary and scientific content and dissemination. On my granddaughter's birthday, I strolled through the Botanical Garden along the Hooghly with Subroto. He took a video of me congratulating the child, so far away in California. In that video, I pretend that I was very close to where my granddaughter was—"close at heart" is the code when loving at a distance.

Slovenia

Slovenia has been named the guest of honor for the 2023 Frankfurt Book Fair. German publishers will present one or two new Slovenian authors in translation to the booksellers, the media, and the readers. In preparation for the event, the Slovenian literary agency under the leadership of Renata Zamida invited small groups of German editors and journalists over the past few years. In June 2017, I was lucky enough to participate in one of those trips since my book on rights and licenses was to be translated into Slovenian and I had some work with the translator. For most of the smaller book markets Germany is the so-called intermediary market. That means when a Slovenian author is translated into the German language, the chances of translations into other European languages increase manifold. Ljubljana, the capital city, is a place for book lovers: bookstores, antiquarian booksellers, and literary academies everywhere; and extensive programs promoting books and reading.

Slovenia, which borders Austria, Hungary, Croatia, and Italy, is a microcosm of the beauty and diversity of Europe. But also of the horrors of the Second World War; the division of the country between Germany, Italy, and Hungary; the massacres and displacement as well as the years in a united socialist Yugoslavia under President Tito; the separation from the Yugoslavian confederation of states with the declaration of independence on June 25, 1991. Recent historical events have left distinct scars in every Slovenian family—of separation, and of political differences. From our conversations with the authors and scientists, we understood that historical events were evermore present now than they had been in the past, as the foundation of the state itself might suggest. The memories find expression in the Slovenian novels, poems, stories, and plays that capture the human condition, the ontological and the metaphysical, in addition to the historical, as every literature in the world does. Without its literature, we may understand nothing of a nation's history or its people. The European continent with its many languages is a special kind of portfolio for translations. The diversity of Slovenia's landscape is supplemented by its culinary diversity which comprises ingredients not only from the region but also Italy, Austria, Croatia, and Hungary.

There were many highlights on that trip. One of them was the dinner with philosopher Slavoj Žižek at Vila Bled Hotel by the lake of the same name. I was given the honor of sitting next to the author. For lack of knowledge of his theories and in great reverence to his intelligence, I managed to steer the conversation toward more personal subjects like marriage and children. Convinced of matrimonial partnerships, both of us agreed that it was sensible to make the marriage proposal as quickly as possible before the proposee changed their mind. We thought it logical that this approach could also lead to multiple marriages.

A year after my first visit to Slovenia, I returned to Vila Bled once more, in June 2018, for a workshop organized by the Slovenian publishers' association. The lake was still cold, and instead of going for a swim I remained sitting on the terrace. The hotel manager came over and said, "Guess who stayed here last week." I suspected none less than Prince Charles because dozens of photos of crowned heads and presidents adorned their beautiful lobby. "No, not Prince Charles but Professor Sauer, who's also from Berlin."—"Chancellor Merkel's husband?" I asked. Yes, was the reply, and with regret she added that they were unaware of this; he was so modest, and had arrived without a security detail. Just as he was leaving, other German guests informed her. The manager was disappointed that I didn't know this famous guest personally even though I was from Berlin; Prof. Sauer had been so friendly to her. She might have thought, then, that my hosts from the publishing business had overexaggerated when they assigned me a status of importance.

Beijing, Shanghai

In the summer of 2004, I touched down in Beijing for the second time in my life. In 1981, I had accompanied a German delegation from the fur industry. And hoped to compare my impressions with those of Simone de Beauvoir from her travels in 1957. But I didn't write a single line after my return to Frankfurt. No one had even expected me to, and unlike Beauvoir I didn't have much to say about China. We had only visited the Forbidden City, the Great Wall, the European city center of Shanghai and concluded the trip in Hong Kong, where the members of the delegation indulged themselves after what seemd like ten days of abstinence in the People's Republic of China. During the three days in Hong Kong, we counted the number of Rolls-Royces on the streets, which made the colonial character of the metropolis even more apparent.

In 2004, I arrived in a completely different country. Shanghai looked more like Manhattan; and Beijing, like Los

Angeles, was crisscrossed by six-lane highways. The retail chains and luxury boutiques that dominated the city centers were the same as in the big European cities; there was a vibrant party scene and live music in the evenings.

The Chinese government had joined the Universal Copyright Convention in 1995. Now there was nothing to impede the selling of translation rights. I arrived at the book fair with an official mission to represent Suhrkamp's German authors, and had scheduled a lot of appointments. Apart from that, Cao Weidong, the translator and colleague of Jürgen Habermas, had invited me to give a presentation on the German publishing industry at Beijing Normal University. I also had the opportunity to visit the publishing houses in Shanghai. This had been my routine every other year until 2010, by when the rights trade between the Chinese and German publishers was firmly established, business relations were consolidated, and Chinese publishers and editors regularly visited the book fairs in Frankfurt and London.

To this day, I find it difficult to define the Chinese book market with respect to the polarity between private industry and state economy. On the one hand, there is censorship on the part of the cultural institutions; on the other, there is the Chinese publishers' openness for and interest in European philosophy and literature together with their extraordinary hospitality. All of this makes the visitor wary of the several aspects. As a trade partner selling rights to German-language works of philosophy and literature in China, I always struggled with commenting on the political system of my host country. Chinese publishers bring out enlightening works by European and American philosophers. The complete editions of critical theory are available in large print runs and the works of Jürgen Habermas, Axel Honneth, and Rainer Forst are an integral part of the curricula in China's faculties of arts and social sciences under a totalitarian regime. This contradiction has fascinated and challenged me throughout my professional life. The departments of German studies and philosophy at Chinese universities are extremely competent. Students and scholars collaborate on translations from other languages. Their language proficiency is excellent, similar to that of many universities in the US, or the Sorbonne, or Oxford and Cambridge. Outside of the publishing houses and the universities, however, understanding the societal and political contexts in China remains a challenge for a visitor.

Chinese publishers have a penchant for complete editions which is also because the length of a German text is shortened by about a third when it is rendered into Mandarin. This rather technical reason is complemented by the care with which the individual work is put into the context of the entire oeuvre. During my time in the rights trade, complete editions of the works of Thomas Bernhard, Paul Celan, Peter Handke, Volker Braun, Hermann Hesse, and Jürgen Habermas were published in China. The deals for the respective collected works were celebrated with aplomb. The dinners were a feast for the senses: various delicacies were placed on a huge revolving plate at the center of the table. Eight courses and ten plates. I was usually the publisher's dinner partner, and with chopsticks he would place each delicacy on my plate—none of which I was familiar with at the beginning of this millennium. The courses and the drinks ranged from the traditional Chinese to globalized variations. Once live crabs had stared me in the face when we celebrated the complete edition of Thomas Bernhard's works; later, however, when it was the works of Paul Celan, my Chinese hosts avoided anything that could disturb their European guest. While there had been copious quantities of Chinese spirits instead of wine as we celebrated the complete edition of Jürgen Habermas's works, years later I was offered an excellent red wine labeled "The Great Wall" when it came to the works of Volker Braun. After the formal dinners, we would dance to live music on the hotels' roof terraces. Over the years, the interior design of the hotels evolved as well: from traditional Chinese to an international, indistinguishable look. The younger generation in the big cities has discovered designer fashion; established successful labels such as Li-Ning; adopted lap dogs; and has very quickly caught up with Silicon Valley and artificial-intelligence technologies. I am not aware of any other society that has achieved such a transformation in the first two decades of the new century.

Beirut, Cairo, United Arab Emirates

Cooperation with the Arab countries began in the late 1990s. With the exception of Libya, all the governments of the different Arab countries had joined the Universal Copyright Convention. Frankfurt Book Fair had invited me to the fair in Beirut. On March 26, 1998, I arrived in the capital of Lebanon. Fifteen years of civil war had ended in 1990, and I hadn't prepared myself to see so many destroyed buildings. I was surprised by the city that was still in the process of being rebuilt, and felt scared that shots could be fired from the ruins that lined the streets throughout the drive from the airport to the city center. In the elegant hotel, at Beirut's seaside promenade, the corniche, I stood sheepishly in the elevator next to women in burkas. We couldn't talk to one another. I also found it difficult to get along with the secular Lebanese women who all looked like Françoise Hardy and stubbed out their cigarettes on lettuce leaves with an air of nonchalance.

At first glance, there seemed to be insurmountable societal differences. On the first night, the German guests had been invited to dine with the media tycoon, diplomat, and author Ghassan Tueni. I met the law professor and human rights activist Chibli Mallat, with whom I remain friends to this day. Sitting at my table were also two philosophy professors from the Christian city of Zahlé in the Beqaa Valley. They knew Suhrkamp's academic non-fiction list better than I did. I was ashamed. But not for long, because the evening was buoyant and sophisticated and outstanding in every regard. The hosts made sure to recommend the choicest Lebanese red wines. In the early hours of the next morning, I looked down from the hotel's roof terrace onto the cedar-covered mountains with snowy peaks on one side and the Mediterranean Sea on the other, and thought to myself: Where have I ever seen anything more beautiful? My worry that I had come to Lebanon at the wrong time faded into the background only to come to the fore again as I entered the room at the book fair for my lecture on foreign rights and licenses. Fifteen publishers from Lebanon and Egypt had taken their seats, and it became clear right away that they had only come to show reverence to the Frankfurt Book Fair which was started in order to uplift the German publishing industry after the civil war and establish a bilateral dialogue with the aid of a collective platform. The publishers listened to me politely, but I got the impression that they would have preferred a man in my place—and in that moment, I would have preferred the same. The discussion revolved mainly around the implementation of copyright measures because the publishers reported pirated copies of their productions in other Arab countries. The Arab book market encompasses many countries that speak the same language; it is the opposite of the multilingual European market. One can imagine great print runs in the Arab-speaking countries, but just as in other parts of the world there is a lack of qualified translators from the German. In the discussion that followed the lecture, we developed several points for cooperation over the course of the following years despite the apparent gender bias.

The attack on the World Trade Center on September 11, 2001, disrupted trade relations between the Arab and the European countries. They didn't come to a complete standstill, but were close to it. It was only in 2004 and 2008 that Arab countries were invited as guests of honor at the Frankfurt Book Fair, and that a number of translations on both sides began to appear again. In addition, publishers, authors, and translators were encouraged to attend conferences in Dubai and the Abu Dhabi Book Fair, and awards with large prize moneys were endowed for translations into Arabic. I visited several fairs and conferences since an exchange with the Arab countries was important to me. It takes decades to get to know one another.

In Cairo, you can't avoid sightseeing—the Nile and the Giza pyramid complex. After the workshop at the Goethe-Institut, I took two days off to see the city and the pyramids. This also included a ride on camelback through the nearby desert. While my driver took me to a cameleer and the two men arranged for a place where the car would pick me up again. The camel was kneeling in the sand, chewing cud. It looked rather old and unenthusiastic about getting up for just one person. It was only when the owner coaxed, "Hey, Champion, it's business time," that the camel allowed me to get on the saddle. I was the camel's "business time." That's not something you get to be every day. The cameleer led the animal through the sand, and I understood why many people feel drawn to desert land-scapes. "This is just like being on the Pacific Ocean," I thought as I floated through the sand. Three hours later, we reached the road where the driver was waiting for me. The men exchanged a few words, then the owner mounted the camel which immediately metamorphosed from slow and elderly to agile and youthful. I let my eyes follow them for a long time.

*Loving
at a Distance*

II

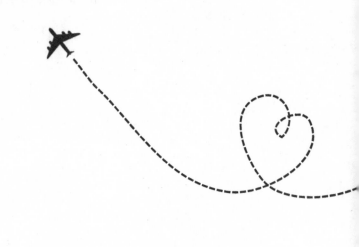

Berkeley

November 2019. After the flight via Greenland and touch-down in San Francisco, I reach my family in Berkeley with my senior ticket on the BART, just in time for Thanksgiving. It's been a week since I retired. Having completed forty years of working life, Suhrkamp gave me a warm goodbye. It wasn't like in Alexander Payne's film *About Schmidt* with Jack Nicholson as the title character. It is based on the Schmidt novels by Louis Begley, where the send-off for a senior employee at an insurance company is downright heartless under the guise of praise. When Schmidt visits his successor three weeks after his departure, he is ushered out politely. Lucky me, I thought on the flight to San Francisco.

In December we are invited to a children's birthday party in San Francisco. On the drive downtown across the Bay Bridge, I think about the years that have gone by. At both times when my grandchildren were born in California, I was at the theater. The nine-hour time difference allows a grandmother to watch plays at the time of the births. In 2014, I was watching Eugène Ionesco's *Le roi se meurt* with my friend Anne Weber at the Théâtre Hébertot in Paris. Michel Bouquet was playing the king. The production by Georges Werler has been performed since 1994. In 1988, my husband and I saw Bouquet in the play *The Miser* by Molière at the same theater. In the 2014 production, Bouquet was better than ever. What a blessing, I thought, to see the same actor at the same theater over the course of decades. After the performance, Anne and I went to Le Wepler restaurant on Place de Clichy and drank a lot of champagne in celebration of the birth of my grandchild. Two years later, during the birth of my grandson, I was with another friend at a performance of *My Fair Lady* at the Komische Oper in Berlin. We celebrated late into the night on the terrace of the Grand Westin. It was summer and everyone was sitting on Gendarmenmarkt and in the restaurants in the surrounding streets. What I appreciate most about having grandchildren is the change in the perception of parental love: You no longer need to explain to your children how much you love them. They already know.

We drive through Mission and Castro, neighborhoods especially affected by gentrification in the last ten years. Evictions are a regular occurrence; the settlements built by the homeless under the urban motorways are growing. I read the many interviews in Cary McClelland's book, *Silicon City: San Francisco in the Long Shadow of the Valley*, with great interest. "Hipsters Out" is plastered on the house fronts in Mission. Rainbow flags are raised above them. Relief organizations temporarily find hospitable families in Berkeley, Albany, and Piedmont for people affected by these developments, and those who have the financial means rent a place somewhere in a different, less expensive part of the city.

The birthday party is in a huge house, like the ones we know from old Hollywood films. Such properties can be maintained only when the responsibility of the upkeep is shared between several families. I don't know anyone at the party. And feel a little out of place since I am the oldest in the group and don't understand what topics the conversations revolve around. Most of the people here work for Twitter or firms specialized in property law. The hostess takes pity on me and says, "Another German grandmother will join us in a moment. She has just stepped outside with her daughter and the baby." Thank God for the other German grandmother. Gaby enters with her grandson in her arm and we begin an intense conversation right away as though we were responsible for the advancement of communication. Not knowing how much time we have to ourselves, we share our life stories in about thirty minutes. Gaby lives near Koblenz, works for a company based in Frankfurt, usually from home, and is just as cheerful and resilient as Barbara Katz Mendes. But I don't mind that this afternoon. We are in the same situation of loving at a distance. We have identical experiences in San Francisco. Even though I'm aware of how impolite it is to talk loudly and am usually the one who finds it rude when two or three people in a group talk in their mother tongue when the others don't understand that language, I enjoyed the hearty chatter with Gaby in German.

Children's birthday parties are always a challenging affair. But it is easier in California. The parents are invited along with their children. This has to do with the distances and the large houses. My children's birthday parties in the Taunus were the only three days a year on which I regretted motherhood. Hosting a multitude of other people's children is difficult. I remember the passage from Max Frisch's *Berlin Journal* where he describes friends with children visiting his apartment. Max is rather annoyed but his wife Marianne is affable. Suhrkamp published that edition the year my granddaughter was born, just in time. Too late for my guilty conscience in the eighties.

The highlight of my hostility toward children, however, was the ninth lantern for a St. Martin's procession that I was asked to make by the kindergarten in Hofheim-Wildsachsen. Three children multiplied by three years of kindergarten added up to nine lanterns for St. Martin's. My suggestion to the kindergarten management to make use of the lantern from the year before was declined, because they had a different theme every year. Up to that point I wasn't aware that there were so many themes around the figure of St. Martin. I also couldn't mention "sustainability," because the word was not part of our everyday vocabulary in the eighties. The kindergarten teacher immediately recognized my aversion to arts and crafts. Both Frisch's *Berlin Journal* as well as the concept of sustainability would have helped me a great deal at the time.

Instead, I drank two glasses of beer in the village hall along with other mothers at the cozy end of the procession.

It's the pre-Christmas time in California and we attend two concerts for children on brilliantly sunny days: one at the Symphony Hall in San Francisco, and the other at the Paramount Theatre in Oakland. All the children in San Francisco are dressed like those of Prince William and Duchess Kate. Which is both odd and beautiful. After the concert, the highlight of which is a celebrated ballet about Mister Grinch, the young visitors can indulge in arts and crafts or eat sweets at different booths in the foyer while the parents are allowed to stroll about.

The Berkeley Children's Theater is showing a wonderful adaptation of the story of "Frog and Toad," based on the books by Arnold Lobel. We also visit the Contra Costa County public library that hosts a puppet show. After we are through with our cultural program for the 2019 Christmas season, I ask my grandchildren which concert or play they enjoyed the most. They both agree it's the puppet show—the only performance that was free.

If I had watched even one sci-fi film in my life before 2019, I would have encountered the Lawrence Hall of Science, the public science center at the University of California, Berkeley. It is one of the locations where *THX1183*, George Lucas' 1971 debut, was filmed. In other sci-fi films it is used as a command center. My daughter-in-law kindly gave me their annual family ticket. At least once a week, the grandchildren and I visit the science center which caters to children between the ages of three and twelve. The children play around and marvel at the displays for hours. The various installations range from dinosaurs to a planetarium; from building dams at the center's garden to using artificial intelligence. At 4 p.m. each day there is a half-hour introduction to the behavior of different animals: we learn about snakes, turtles, snails, spiders, parrots. The center shuts its doors to visitors at 5 p.m., that's when my grandchildren and the other kids climb on to the huge whale in front of the hall as I watch the sunset over the Golden Gate Bridge and San Francisco. These are the moments of unbridled happiness.

At least once during my stay in Berkeley, I drive to Silicon Valley, to Menlo Park, Palo Alto, or to Stanford University. In November 2019, professors Hans Ulrich Gumbrecht and Robert P. Harrison invited me to the philosophical seminar they organized on the occasion of German philosopher Peter Sloterdijk's visit. Prof. Harrison is an expert on narrative structures; he advises his students to "read Boccaccio's *Decameron* and learn the art of storytelling by yourself." He is critical of the content on streaming services and the fact that we are losing the art of oral narratives, of "novellare." At the time of the seminar, we had no inkling of the imminent coronavirus pandemic. During the pandemic many people around the world recommended reading books by Boccaccio, Camus, García Márquez, and Manzoni. Before the seminar began, I visited an exhibition organized by art students in the university's Art Hall. And especially liked the exhibit by Annie Ng titled *Me and Mine*—a collection of ten digital prints through which the artist expresses her cultural dysphoria. Born a Chinese woman in Hong Kong with a British education, she perceives herself as a "banana, yellow on the outside and white on the inside, yellow face and colonialism." For the artist, this series is "an expression of longing for belonging," as the descriptions explain. After the seminar, the students, teachers, and guests dine at an Arab restaurant in Menlo Park. Here I meet the representatives of the Austrian cultural forum in San Francisco. We immediately start making plans for an intercultural dialogue between Europe and the Valley. Each of us contributes their personal experience. I recommend getting the American Literary Translators Association (ALTA) on board with us.

I had been invited to the conference "Celebrating the Past / Imagining the Future" on the occasion of ALTA's thirtieth anniversary at the University of Texas in Dallas from November 7 to 10, 2007, by the comparatist Rainer Schulte who had obtained his PhD in Michigan in 1965 for a thesis on Henry James and Marcel Proust. The conference entailed four days of discussions between the American translators who work across twenty different languages apart from English and guests from other cultural sectors.

The staff members of the Austrian cultural forum agreed on another meeting in March 2020 (which would end up getting canceled because of the pandemic).

In December 2019, we participate in two excursions at my granddaughter's school. First, we go to the Botanical Gardens behind the campus in Berkeley. I am allowed to come along since my name is on the list of potential chaperones. At the Botanical Gardens, the sixteen pupils of the class are divided into four groups. Each group is provided with a retired biology teacher. They talk in detail about the plants and redwoods, and explain how the stream meandering through the garden is connected to the trees. What a luxury, I think: four children and one lecturer. Over the course of the tour, the lecturer asks me which of the four children was my granddaughter. At first, I think she's having me on, but then I realize that she is being serious. Of course, it could by any one of the children there, I just didn't get it at first. But I did learn my lesson! Just as I do each time I visit the fitness club at the YMCA in downtown Berkeley: they have a significantly more polyethnic group than in comparable clubs in Germany. Exchange programs, I think: more state-run and private exchange programs for both teenagers and older people.

I signed up to introduce my profession at the Career Day event in my granddaughter's school, even though I haven't been actively working for three months. I'm going to present as a "Publisher." That hasn't been done in the sessions in the past. Would I be able to recommend a profession that is not so common in Silicon Valley? Hope I don't fail. Here in the

East Bay Area in California, the "narratives" are of an entirely different character.

The February of 2020 is a particularly sunny and warm month in Northern California. The magnolias are in full bloom. The view of the Golden Gate Bridge, downtown San Francisco, Sausalito, and the bay from the Berkeley Hills in the early light of the year is breathtaking. San Francisco advertises itself as the most beautiful city in the world. Such ascriptions are allowed but not very sensible considering the thousands of places around the globe that could claim the same. My granddaughter and I will go to a family concert at the San Francisco Symphony Hall as soon as I arrive.

My parents didn't care for the art form of opera. My father did have a nice baritone and might occasionally belt out the aria of the Hunters' Choir from Weber's *Der Freischütz* or Figaro's aria from *The Barber of Seville*, but the singing was too loud for my mother; she always complained. Due to her long stays at various sanatoriums, everything was too loud for my mother. Even the clattering of my fork against the plate was too noisy. My father used to say that the performers at the opera sang the text two or three times louder so that they could be heard even in the last row. He also made fun of the opera audience, who were, according to him, stuffy. But he said it in a way that let me develop a sense of freedom to not only fall in love with the operatic form but also visit Frankfurt Opera as soon as I was able.

My paternal grandmother loved Wagner. He was a Nazi, my mother had said. It took me years to overcome my inhibitions about listening and understanding Wagner. On Christmas 1963, I was presented with a record with arias from Mozart's *Magic Flute*. I played it incessantly and fell in love with Walter Berry as Papageno.

The Old Opera at the end of Große Bockenheimer Straße, the so-called Alley of Gluttony, was in ruins in the 1960s. The local parties and citizens were arguing about the restoration. From 1951 to 1960 the Opera was hosted at the former theater. Those were the years when Georg Solti helped the Frankfurt Opera regain its reputation. Despite the new home on what would become Willy Brandt Platz, there were countless initiatives to rebuild the Old Opera and so the students of the sixth grade at the Heinrich von Gagern Grammar School received an appeal to conduct a donation drive. First prize was a VW Beetle. I wasn't expecting winning the first prize. Almost all residents of Frankfurt-Bornheim had an even greater dislike for the opera than my parents or they weren't interested in art and music at all and had no funds to spare for cultural spaces. They considered the project very expensive and a waste of financial resources. Despite knowing all of this, I roamed around Bornheim with my collection tin. I thought it was much more sensible to collect donations for the opera than for the Müttergenesungswerk (Maternity Recovery Service) which I had done earlier. And for that you had to give someone a flower after they had made a donation and my best friend and I fought over who got to hold the tin and who handed out the flowers. Beyond that, I didn't understand the purpose of the Recovery Service because my mother was exhausted not from the number of children or the housework but from her illness and the Nazis. My father continued to do the housework and the two of us were very considerate of her. I would have seen more use in collecting donations for a charity dedicated to the well-being of the children and their fathers. And now the Old Opera.

Our class teacher had shown us pictures of what the opera had looked like when it had first opened in 1880. It was beautiful. I imagined Walter Berry performing there and me in the audience. That was motivation enough. We had three weeks' time and after that we had to hand in the tins with our names on them. Three weeks, hither and thither. Löwengasse, upper Bergstraße, Buchaldstraße, Inheidener Straße. The first 500 children who had collected the most amount were invited to an event at the New Opera House. My name was on the list too, and not in a bad position at all: I came 379th. My father accompanied me to the event and even though they only performed three arias from three operas, I knew that this is where I wanted to be forever. The three sons of the head of the surgery at the university hospital in Frankfurt came first and won the VW Beetle. They had collected donations from affluent neighborhoods and at the hospital. I generously applauded my fellow student and his brothers. I knew that my achievement was definitely tantamount to theirs: making to the 379th place with a collection drive in Frankfurt-Bornheim. After we got home that evening, my father had said, "I think our child should learn to play an instrument." My mother had replied, "Perhaps a quiet one if anything—because of the neighbors."I decided on the flute because of Walter Berry.

Most of the public schools in Berkeley seem like private schools. It is amazing what they offer to the children with regard to courses, excursions, but especially the after-school programs for the so-called kindergarteners. On my grand-daughter's first day of school, I was confused by the fact that first grade is called kindergarten. From pre-school at the day-care center the children move to kindergarten at the ele-mentary school; it took some time for me to understand that, particularly since there are regional differences in terminology. So that's what migration feels like, and I think of the grand-mothers in Berlin's Wedding. It's impossible to assess and con-textualize the things you have understood. Worse still, you often can't even gauge what you have or haven't understood. This exacerbates my insecurity. I ask so many questions of my surroundings every day although with restraint so as not to exhaust the aura of the German grandmother in the Bay Area. My special status also results from the fact that only a few of the conversations I have in the Bay Area are with people my age. I talk about politics with the neighbors who put up "Bernie Sanders" signs in February 2020, ahead of Super Tuesday; about exercise with the ladies at the gym; about the weather with the churchgoers on Sundays. Those conversations are but a few sentences with approachable Americans. We live in different worlds. The first time I attended a service at St. Mary Magdalen Church in Berkeley, the priest looked in my direction at the end of the service and said that there were visitors in their midst and could they please stand up and introduce themselves. After I shared where I was from, the congregation gave me a great applause. That's the custom. What a hospitable country! I thought. However, up until now, no friendships have resulted from these encounters. My temporary residence permit prevents any possible long-term connections. Which I completely understand. You need to participate in the social events and get-togethers round the year in order to build friendships.

Why is my role as a migrating grandmother constantly occupying my mind? I'm insecure. Try as I might, I can't make up for the sixty years that a grandmother who was born in California has. No one expects that of me, I know. But I want to belong, too. I'm embarrassed that my grandchildren have a grandmother who wasn't born in the city they call home. Even though that is the case for seventy-five percent of their classmates, my wish to blend in seems to be greater than that of other grandparents from around the world. The two Indian grandmothers who I got to know a bit better, both originally from my beloved Kolkata, are more relaxed about it. They aren't trying to assimilate into American society.

In early March 2020, the afternoon group of the kindergarteners at the Berkeley Arts Magnet School had a meeting with Mayor Jesse Arreguín (Democrat). The children asked questions about the coronavirus and about the presidential election. The various departments of the mayor's office introduce themselves briefly. And they inform the group that everyone is concerned with keeping the apartments and houses in Berkeley affordable for the teachers, the hospital employees, and to spare them the fate of the people in Mission and Castro. While the visionaries in Silicon Valley spend resources on designing socially relevant products, the people around them scramble for a suitable cave like in the Stone Age. Machines will become intelligent and more socially relevant only when basic human needs are met. Which shouldn't be all that hard—what with the ability of artificial intelligence to analyze data, determine patterns, and create predictive models.

The complexity of the Bay Area with the Valley is confusing and fascinating every time: with the vast beaches along the Pacific, the redwood forests, the city of San Francisco with its winners of the digital age, their suppliers' empire, the army of service providers, and the smaller cities like Sausalito, Berkeley, Richmond, Oakland, all of which have their very own characters. There are millions of interesting individual cases, many of which I have been tracing and discarding over the past decade. I am in a constant state of reconciliation.

The SARS-CoV-2 virus has now reached California. A cruise ship is held in quarantine in Oakland. I have decided not to attend the Patti Smith concert scheduled on March 9 at Fillmore Hall. I was looking forward to it for months. I always wanted to watch Patti Smith perform in San Francisco and not in Berlin where she performs once a year. The concert goes on without me. My friend Barbara Katz Mendes, who had booked the tickets for us, was undeterred. Once more, I envy her nonchalance. But I take advice from Germany which issued an advisory stating that all we can do to prevent the viral transmission is to avoid mass events. Many events are being canceled in Berkeley, including the Career Day at the Berkeley Arts Magnet School that was scheduled for mid-March. I had enthusiastically signed up to give a talk about careers in publishing back in January, but was not sure how to interest the students aged between ten and fourteen in such matters. Now the cancellation—a relief.

The situation is becoming worse by the day. President Trump has decided to no longer let Europeans into the country. We fear that all flights to Europe will be canceled too. I will have to leave the US a month earlier than planned. While we are deliberating on my return flight, we receive the message that schools in the Bay Area are going to shut. We explain to my granddaughter that we will have to reschedule her sixth birthday party, which she had been eagerly looking forward to. And I tell her how I, too, had to put off my birthday once.

My mother had said, "We're going to have to postpone your birthday party—President John F. Kennedy is going to visit Germany." President Kennedy came to Frankfurt on June 25, 1963—the day of my ninth birthday—before going on to make his historic speech in Berlin a day later. He was driven from

Hanau to Frankfurt in an open-top Mercedes. My parents and
I stood at the riverbank of the Main near the cathedral for two
hours before the convoy finally arrived; and within about ten
seconds, he had moved past the cheering crowd. I didn't really
get to see him, even though my father had lifted me in his arms.
My parents, particularly my mother, were enthusiastic fans of
the US and the American way of life. After the war, my mother
had worked as a nanny for an American family in Heidelberg
(she had to quit that job in 1949, unfortunately, due to her illness). That's why she could speak English very well, which was
not typical for her generation. "We owe the Americans everything, absolutely everything," she used to say. "And De Gaulle
and Churchill," my father would add. But my parents were not
just enthralled by American politics: the music, the lifestyle—
everything was better, they believed. By the time they were able
to go on long trips to the US, they were in their mid-forties.
They had hung up a large map of the United States in our
kitchen, and every year they would add colorful pins to mark
the places they visited. We ended up celebrating my birthday
on June 26 that year. And like every year, we had strawberry
cake, hedgehog slice, Frankfurters, and potato salad, and
my father performed magic tricks for our six guests and me.
My friends brought me crayons and a boardgame called
Deutschlandreise (Trip to Germany) which we then played
without pause. The GDR didn't exist on the map of the game
but Lake Titi in the Black Forest did. The lake was lined by
dark firs. On the evening of November 22, 1963, my mother
cried after she heard of the President Kennedy's assassination

in Dallas. "At least you got to see him," she said. I didn't, but that was not important at the time.

We are all feeling unsafe. And we go into the fight mode. We try to encourage one another, keep our spirits up. We imagine the virus as a monster. My grandson brings out his lightsaber. The universe strikes back.

That which I feared the most has happened. The pandemic has caused an involuntary separation from those I love. We don't live on the same continent. We can't walk toward each other, or so much as wave at each other. We need the help of technology to see one another. And even though we have some command over it, loving at a distance is a challenge. When we are being controlled by others, the entire inventory of approaches we have carefully designed fails us. I have experienced painful separations as a child. That is of no help now. Sixty years lie between the separation from my mother then and from my grandchildren now.

Until the age of six I was raised by my father, aunt and grandparents; my mother was mostly absent, having fallen ill with tuberculosis and was usually at the sanatorium. When she was with us, there was a lot of tears, and my mother had to be put to sleep. I had to be quiet all the time: a quiet, reading child.

Before I learnt to read, I had, in addition to my many picture books, consumed my parents' illustrated volumes on Naples and Sicily, bibliophilic editions published by the Büchergilde book club. My favorite image was that of a Neapolitan family sitting together at the table—twenty people of different generations. At our table there were just two, my father and me. My father and the books. Those were the pillars of my childhood.

My father was an entertainer, a squanderer of emotions and money. Some of our good days would compensate for an entire Neapolitan clan. He worked for the trade magazine of an auto club and on the weekends he got to test drive various makes and models. In summer, the two of us would drive to Heidelberg to see my mother's parents, refugees from Gdansk. Her father had gone mute on account of two world wars and the loss of his homeland; he only spoke a few sentences in the evening after enjoying some sweet Rhine wine or a liquor called Danziger Goldwasser. My grandmother, on the other hand, would just say, "Oh, the poor child!" every time we arrived. My aunt Anita's mood ranged from being cheerful to traumatized. She smoked and drank, and had a long-term fiancé whom my mother called a Nazi. I had lived with my grandparents and aunt for a whole year and only seen my father on the weekends until he brought me back to Frankfurt. I had almost forgotten my mother during that time. In that so-called Heidelberg Year, my grandparents would send my thirty-year-old aunt and me to church every Sunday. They would have already been to early Mass. While we were away, my grandmother prepared the family lunch. It was a usual fare of duck, goose, carp, or pike, like they would have in Gdansk.

Later, I was surprised to learn that other families would only have these dishes for Christmas. We never made it to the church though, as one of Anita's older colleagues lived en route to St. Boniface. The ladies drank sparkling wine and smoked cigarettes. I would sip on my orange juice and play with the cat. Since the cat didn't quite enjoy my company, I would spend time observing the son of Anita's friend from the corner of my eye instead; he was a medical student and remained immersed in his books.

Our non-attendance at Mass was unnoticed, until my grandmother and I ran into the chaplain at the weekly market and he expressed surprise that I was in Heidelberg. Anita had by then found work as a store clerk at a shop on Heidelberg's main street that sold expensive furniture and trinkets. When she returned home that evening, there was a heated exchange between mother and daughter and I heard my aunt say "Bible thumpers," and grandmother mention "the wrath of God." The following Sunday, the four of us went to the main Mass at ten in the morning followed by lunch. We could not, however, continue this as one has to be sober to receive communion, but my grandfather was unable to abstain on account of his physical and emotional injuries.

After church, I would see my father. On Saturdays, he would drive to the Black Forest to visit his wife at the sanatorium, and on his way back the next day he stopped to see his child. He spent the entire day with us and would not leave for Frankfurt until late, when I was asleep. On Monday mornings, I would stare at my picture books. Sometimes I cried, and when I did, Anita would say, "Don't cry, I'll buy you some chocolate cigarettes." We would walk to the bakery and smoke. Anita, her Stuyvesant; I, my chocolate cigarettes. Which was surely more difficult than smoking the Stuyvesants, because the paper dissolved in my mouth and I had to swallow it along with the chocolate.

After a year of weekend trips, my father had had enough and brought me back to Frankfurt. He moved my mother to a sanatorium in Bad Homburg. Anita would come to Frankfurt every Saturday and visit us. After I returned, she moved in with her fiancé in Mannheim. At four o'clock, she would step off the train onto Platform 8. In the summer, she would wear a white skirt suit, a carton of Peter Stuyvesant sticking out of her white leather purse. My father and I would drive to the station an hour before her train arrived. First, we'd feast on Frankfurters, then go to the AKI, the cinema with continuous screenings that changed every twenty-four hours. News and English-language serials in which policemen with German shepherds arrested thieves and sex criminals. It was very dark and eerie; the usher used her flashlight to guide the patrons to their unnumbered seats. Homeless people, prostitutes, and travellers occupied most of the seats. It smelt of urine and nicotine. But I was happy. I had my father all to myself; I was yet to learn to share him with someone else.

I had been waiting for my mother for years. When she was finally returned home for good, she had changed. Once, as we were walking to Platform 8 after going to the cinema, a steam locomotive arrived on Platform 1. People with a lot of luggage got off the train. My father bent down toward me, and whispered, "That's the train from East Germany." I thought that it was a country where only old people lived, since I wasn't aware that only the older citizens could obtain a travel permit. This impression was intensified by our annual visits to the parents of my aunt's fiancé, whom my mother also called Nazis. Hilde and Egon were old. At Christmas, they came from Hoyerswerda to Mannheim, where their son worked at a Ford dealership. The fact that they had been Nazis was disclosed only by my mother, but that they looked like everyone else who had just got off the train on Platform 1 was more obvious. They were nice to me. Egon had survived various political systems as head accountant of a coal mine in the Lausitz region. Hilde sang Christmas songs in a high soprano. At Christmas, they joined us in Frankfurt: the grandparents from Heidelberg, Anita, and her fiancé, Ehrenfried, along with his parents. I was the only child in the group. And there I sat, among the traumatized people, thinking all of this was completely normal: all those quarrels between Hilde and my grandmother, Agnes; their husbands' futile attempts at placating them; and my mother's constant blaming of everything on the Nazis. My uncle slipped away as often as possible; he visited every branch of Ford–General Motors in Frankfurt and Offenbach. First, he took his own Ford to the Americans in Adickesallee, then he drove on to the Gallus neighborhood and to Fechenheim. My mother blamed his parents, "That's because you raised him like a Nazi. Instead of listening to the Pope's 'Urbi et Orbi' blessing on the radio, he goes out to see his cars." My mother didn't take note of the fact that my uncle's family was Protestant and thus didn't put too much importance on the Pope's blessing. For her, everything was either for or against the Nazis. I withdrew with my new book. My uncle had given me an illustrated children's edition of the Odyssey. Penelope became the shining light of my first year of school. Waiting for someone, for one's mother and father, was something I had learned from my own early life. Waiting twenty years for a man seemed completely reasonable to me. That was Christmas 1961; I couldn't have known then that all of those experiences would help me decades later with loving at a distance.

The last four days before my flight to Germany are sad and hectic. The adults are trying to put on a brave face. They are shutting down not only the schools in the Bay Area but also the libraries, the Lawrence Hall of Science, the children's theater, the playgrounds. My grandchildren and I return all the books to Contra Costa County Library. "See you soon and stay healthy," said the librarians, reassuringly. Afterward, we go to one of our favorite places in Berkeley: Mr. Mopps' Toy Shop. I buy far too many things for the grandchildren: eight books, Legos, necklaces, and knick-knacks from the counter next to the cash register—kowtowing to the kids' "*May I have this too?*" Before we say goodbye, they *may have* anything they please. I would bring along the whole shop with us if I could. On the evening before and the morning of my flight, we read all the books aloud, again and again. I'm miserable. I read aloud with extra cheer in my voice.

Loving
at a Distance

III

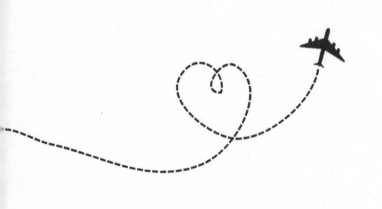

In the Virtual Space
between Berlin and Berkeley

The pandemic has also separated other families. And that gives me comfort. The virus isolates everyone spatially. Not just those who live on different sides of the Atlantic. Communication is entirely via online apps. I am well versed in that: I could write a manual on how to talk to one's grandchildren online. Especially those aged between two and six. The more traditional puppet theater—we used to have Punch-and-Judy shows when I was a child—is suitable for children between three and six. Reading a book aloud is a good option for all ages before they learn to read themselves. For your online reading session, you will need to have two copies of the book so that you can hold the illustrations up to the screen and read the text from the second copy, or you will have to make do with one copy and scan the text and share, or you can make a video of the book and the text. The bookseller in Kladow, Herr Kuhnow, once said to me at the cash register: "You already have that book." I needed two copies for Skype, I had replied. He looked at me, astonished. He doesn't have grand-children in California.

Arts and crafts, cutting, gluing and kneading also work splendidly via Skype, or other similar apps. You need every-thing in duplicate. We also play with dolls. I still have the dolls Bärbel and Edith and so we can play together on screen.

Recently, Herr Kuhnow gave me a book which was designed for booksellers by Carlsen Verlag. It tells the story of how a family goes to a local bookstore where the book-seller, mentioned by name, recommends the right book for each family member. Herr Kuhnow recommends a book about "the brave cow" for the family's daughter, which had my granddaughter and me in fits of laughter. She asked, "Does that book really exist?" I promised to find an answer to this important question when I return to Berlin. And as promised, I went to see Herr Kuhnow; he quietly smiled and recom-mended the Mama Moo series originally published in Swedish. I chose two copies of *Mama Moo Reads* for our reading ses-sion on Skype. After our conversation on books with cows, we create unicorns, and penguins from Plasticine; and the dolls in Berkeley talk to the dolls in Berlin. And after all this, I must take refuge in Hölderlin; I think German actor Jens Harzer's readings of Hölderlin's *Hyperion* is beautiful to listen to. But what I appreciate the most about children is that they require skills that have nothing to do with the world of grown-ups. One enjoys returning to them and to their world more often, for their world is a haven for grown-ups.

The only friends I had during my stays in the Bay Area over the course of the past ten years come from South America. Barbara Katz Mendes was born in Venezuela, is an economist and came to wealth in the United States. Her children live in Texas and Australia. She is also not sure when she will see her four grandchildren again. Physician and teacher Isabel Philips is from Honduras. She has her children and grandchildren who live with her in Berkeley. She manages the after-school programs at the Berkeley Arts Magnet School. Her work is praiseworthy: she organizes exhibitions of books and paintings; Spanish lessons; meeting with the mayor; and excursions to the university. I have been in touch with both of them since my involuntary return to Berlin. Isabel writes that in-person classes won't be possible for the 2020 academic year, and that the session will be conducted entirely online. What will that do to the children who have only just begun to learn to read, write, and do math? How will this affect those who have only just learned to find their bearings in a school community? What are such restrictions doing to our children and grandchildren? We won't be able to predict the long-term consequences yet.

The memories of the evening spent with Isabel at the overcrowded César, a tapas bar in North Berkeley, seem from another life, although it has only been three weeks. It is amazing how many people can already describe the life after the pandemic, and how societies are going to change over time. But I really don't know. Neither does Jürgen Habermas. In an interview with the *Frankfurter Rundschau,* he says: "Our complex societies are constantly encountering great insecurities, but they occur locally and not at the same time . . . and are . . . processed in subsystems of society. Now, on the other hand, an existential insecurity is spreading globally and simultaneously." And from this he concludes: "There has never been as much knowledge about what we don't know and about the pressure of having to act and live with our insecurities." I conclude for our family that life on two continents or loving at a distance won't be getting any easier. In normal times we Skype once a week; it has become more frequest during the pandemic. We will have a painting competition via Skype; the subjects are varied: a princess, flowers in a pot, a propeller, and a mermaid. Don't know why I suggested the mermaid when I'm not good at drawing anyway. But I did buy new colored pencils which I keep on my table so that we can begin straight-away when my grandchildren call.

There hasn't been any rain in Berlin for weeks. I look at my umbrella stand with three umbrellas and feel sad. We will soon experience other, more severe problems than just the SARS-CoV-2 virus. And everyone knows it, too.

My grandchildren send me nice videos. I'm not very sure what I should record for them. Nothing has been happening here since mid-March 2020. I sit at home in Gatow or in the garden by the Havel. It's not easy to take a video of what is happening around me or how I feel about it. So I'm going to ride my bike to Kladow and ask Herr Kuhnow if I could film inside the bookstore. Books is all I can do. And Netflix. I have been watching the *Blacklist* series for hours during the so-called lockdown. Actor James Spader is superb in his role as the suave criminal Raymond Reddington! A thriller that exults in crime, murder, betrayal, revenge, oaths of allegiance, a mysterious relationship between father and daughter—and full of quotations from world literature. Without the seven seasons of *Blacklist*, I wouldn't have survived the lockdown as well as I did.

The longing grows. By now, it's autumn and we still don't know when we can see each other again. A different emotion sneaks in and melds with the longing for the family on the other continent: the longing for Berkeley, San Francisco, and Menlo Park. I'm astonished. Perhaps, I understood more about these cities than I wanted to acknowledge? Are there places of longing now in California just as there are in France—places to which I keep wanting to return? The so-called Food Area in North Berkeley seems like paradise to me. The restaurant Chez Panisse, famous with many people the world over, is at the center of the lively neighborhood. Alice Waters and Paul Aratow founded the legendary restaurant in 1971. The name is a homage to Honoré Panisse, the cheerful character from the Marseille trilogy by Marcel Pagnol—based on his novels, *Souvenirs d'enfance*. Not far from there is Saul's Deli where you can eat kosher and non-kosher dishes; my grandchildren and I love the matzah there. Large photos of Jewish weddings hang on the walls, of bar mitzvahs and bat mitzvahs. Next to Saul's Deli is Books Inc., "The West's Oldest Independent Bookseller," with eleven branches and two hundred employees and a fascinating history of bankruptcies and recoveries—an essentially American story. The gourmet mile along Shattuck Avenue, toward downtown Berkeley, also houses an ice-cream shop with a name that spans an arc from Early Italian baroque to artificial intelligence: Caravaggio Gelato Lab. Apart from the traditional choices they have rare flavours such as matcha green tea, black sesame, or caramelized peach. On our last visit to the shop, my grand-daughter wanted melon. It wasn't in stock at the time. The owner promised to make it sooner than usual for her so that we would be able to have it together before I left for Berlin. It usually takes five days to make the ice cream, from sourcing the ingredients to chilling it until the customers can buy the flavor of their choice. California is exemplary when it comes to producing organic food through healthy and transparent processes.

I am in touch with our neighbors in Berkeley and with my two friends. They are all happy that Joe Biden has chosen as his running mate Senator Kamala Harris—a woman from Oakland: one of them. One of the neighbors writes that she can hear the grandchildren laugh in the garden. How much I envy her! Loving at a distance is full of risks. I think about the little girl at my grandson's kindergarten who used to cry a lot. I tried to comfort her at times. But the teacher said, "She doesn't understand any English—only Finnish and French." So I spoke to her in French which sometimes helped calm the flood of tears. I learned that her mother was conducting a six-month-long research at the university. That little Finnish girl who spoke French so well only because her mother had worked at the Sorbonne before coming to Berkeley—where would she be now?

My third grandchild is born in June 2020 in Northern Baden, close to my ancestors' multigenerational house in Wiesloch. I visit Mirko B. to get a tattoo of the newborn girl's initials.

Freshly tattooed, I read an interview in the *Süddeutsche Zeitung* with the director of the Berliner Festspiele, Thomas Oberender, one of the best culture managers in Europe. The interview revolves around the newly opened exhibition entitled "Down to Earth" in reference to the book of the same name by the French philosopher Bruno Latour. The exhibition combines art and ecological experiments. "We have left the Anthropocene and have arrived in the age of planetary worry," says Oberender. I agree with him.

Wildfires are raging in California again. This time the entire Bay Area is surrounded, both north of Berkeley as well as the south of San José. The sky oscillates between orange and black. The apocalyptic images travel around the world. There are days when climate change comes calling and planetary worry becomes more personal. The pain of separation and the insecurity about what is to come affects us all, and each of us in their own way.

I drive to the Theater am Rand at Oderaue, near the border with Poland. The director Thomas Rühmann is reading Julio Cortázar's 1966 short story "The Southern Thruway," in a scenic and musical production. The allegorical story describes how a traffic jam on the southern Boulevard Périphérique in Paris, which lasts for months not hours, forces people to question the basics of human existence with consequences similar to what we are observing during the pandemic. Rühmann reads wonderfully. I return to Berlin invigorated.

After the matinee at the Theater am Rand, I Skype with my grandchildren. They are growing up, learning to swim, doing math, and reading without my immediate presence. They are even encouraging their grandmother by putting together a list of all the things we are going to do post-pandemic. They will be able to read to me by then. The world has turned upside down.

Now more that ever, I understand that I need my grandchildren more than they need me. I learn how much the dates of our reunions in the countdown app carry me through life. At my departure in March, I had entered "Thanksgiving 2020" into the app to comfort my grandmother-soul, and I'm now forced to delete it again. The distance cancels out the simultaneity of the time of day, the season, the language, the habits. The simultaneity of love cannot be dissolved.

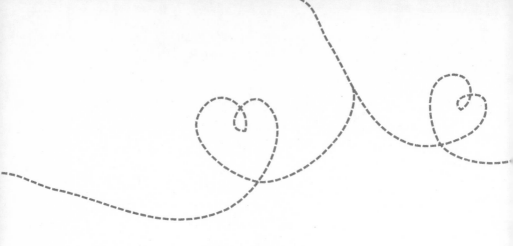

Acknowledgments

I have been working closely with Naveen Kishore for over fifteen years. Literary authors around the world have much to thank him for. Honored with prestigious awards, and deservedly so, Naveen and his team at Seagull Books make decisions in favor of literature, diversity, and independence. This volume focuses on long-distance love and our lives in books, and seeing it published by Seagull is more than I could have expected in my lifetime. And I thank Naveen Kishore, Sunandini Banerjee, Bishan Samaddar, and Sayoni Ghosh from the bottom of my heart. My thanks to Laura Wagner for her translation, and to Nora Mercurio for her very kind and efficient support.

*

At the time of writing, the Lebanese publishing house Al Kamel published the Arabic translation of this volume. Publisher Khalid Al Maaly worked on it so quickly that I didn't get the chance to revise the acknowledgments in their edition—Naveen is generous enough to give me the space here—so I would like to take this opportunity to express my sincere thanks to Khalid Al Maaly, translator Hebba Sherif, and Felix Dahm for all their work.

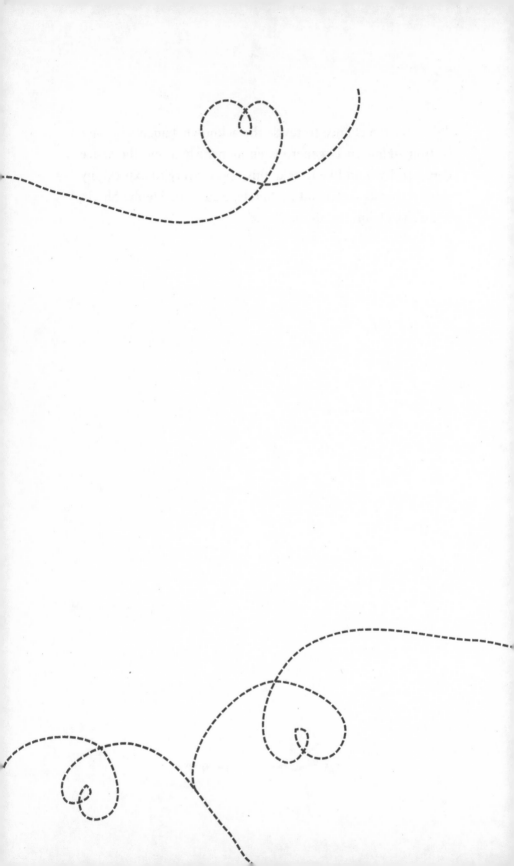